My Soul Longs for You, My God

A Collection of Poetry

Matthew R. Goldammer

Table of Contents

God the Father, embrace us as Your children.

God the Son, have mercy on us, sinners.

God the Holy Spirit, enflame our hearts with Your love.

And Blessed Mother Mary, carry us always to your Son.

Amen.

Introduction

When the Lord fills the heart with a song so sweet that everything else is consumed by its grandeur, the heart bursts forth such joy beyond description that there is nothing that can contain the echo of that song that it sings with all its strength. Neither the heart nor the mind alone can begin to grasp this divine melody, and they together only unravel but a figment of its true nature. The Mind that is God, unmovable in being, thinks of His creation at all times; ah, the symphony He has made, and how it permeates all with His love! Man has a unique perspective in the universe to be formed in God's image and likeness, and yet still lack the capacity to perceive his Creator directly. Thus, the Lord enlightens the ears of man to the divine song that is His love according to His will. Man's response, then, is either to listen to the Lord or ignore Him.

This is the state in which we find ourselves at every moment, potentially able to hear the voice of God if we are but tranquil and still, ready to receive what He desires to tell us. How eloquent is this silence through which the Lord chooses to speak: truly how subtle, and yet direct; how gentle, and yet powerful all the same. Through this silence we learn to dwell with Him. Through this silence our souls are lifted to Him, immersed in His eternal and everlasting song of love.

The gaze of the Lord in the Blessed Sacrament is undoubtedly so intense and powerful that a soul, if open to His promptings, is moved with such joy when seeing God from behind the sacramental veil. This piercing tranquility guides the soul to move beyond itself, not forced but rather gently raised by the Lord above the perceptions of the exterior senses to a place within that defies description.

Ah, the interior sweetness when removed from time and placed with such delicacy on the breast of Jesus Christ, listening to His Sacred Heart beat the steady pulse of perfect love for each one of us! How impeccable are the ways of God, that He can guide every soul to this peace. There is no soul in the world deficient of this capacity within – God has crafted each soul with His own hands, gifting each with the potential to know Him intimately, and thus love Him with every fiber of its being. Only an unwilling disposition, poisoned by sin, can prevent this union from transpiring, and this is done by the soul's gradual disobedience. Every person is guilty of this disobedience, for no human being is perfect. But the story of humanity does not end with our sinfulness, for God the Father sent His only Son, Jesus, for our salvation – in humble gratitude, then, let us praise God for His mercy and forgiveness! It brings joy and hope to know that despite our failures God still loves us. We cannot earn His love; He loves us just as we are.

With this internal disposition of yearning for the Kingdom of God, we can go forward in life ready to improve morally so that we might be deemed worthy of Himself when God calls us home at death. Whenever that day is, God only knows. Relying on the help of God for the journey, we turn to His Son, our Lord Jesus Christ, and cling to Him. Our hearts rejoice that we are members of His body; we are one in Christ.

Praised be Jesus Christ. Now and forever. Amen.

God the Father, embrace us as Your children.
God the Son, have mercy on us, sinners.
God the Holy Spirit, enflame our hearts with Your love.
And Blessed Mother Mary, carry us always to your Son.

Amen.

Part 1

The Power of Scripture

When we encounter scripture, we enter into an experience of spiritual intimacy with the Word of God, Jesus Christ. This intimacy with the Son of the Father transcends any human boundaries that man has established on earth, and through it we receive a greater understanding of the Triune God through the working of the Holy Spirit, the true Author of scripture from the beginning.

There is growing darkness in the world, and due to the corresponding increase of violence – physically, emotionally, and spiritually – man finds it easier to lose hope. What follows from that is not that he loses hope *de facto*, but with the adversity he faces it is unavoidably more possible that that unfortunate outcome of losing hope could come. Ironically, this seemingly human problem does not inherently originate in man himself, but in man's *choice* to sin. This decision does not define him, but rather indicates a change in direction from the path of righteousness to the path that leads to self-destruction: sin can never create; it only destroys.

Thus, even in man's tendency to sin inherited from Adam and Eve's fall (see Genesis 3), he still remains a free being, created in God's image and likeness (cf. Genesis 1:26-27). Man is a human being, not a human "doing." If he were only defined by doing, then the measure of a person would be dependent on how he has succeeded in life, and nothing more. Furthermore, the committing of moral acts is contingent upon one's interior disposition. If one is open to the Lord and seeks to serve Him in his life, then the grace that God gives is already at work within him. Contrarily, if one pushes away the Lord's gentle invitations to living a life of virtue and love, then it is very difficult to see the light of the Lord's grace shining forth from him or her because of the repeated denials of the Lord's mercy. Ultimately, it is dangerously easy for sin to enter our lives; we all need Christ's love and forgiveness each and every day. With Him, there is always hope! Indeed, Peter denied even knowing Jesus *three times* (see John 18:15-27), but eventually he accepted the Lord's mercy and forgiveness in response to a growing repentance of heart: an interior disposition of fertile soil for the Lord to plant seeds of goodness in his soul.

In all things, man must first realize his incredible capacity within himself, given by God, *to understand, love, and serve.* From the efficacy of the catalyst of his interior freedom, both inherently from God and also from himself by habitual behavior, man finds himself the holder of his destiny within the context of God's eternal plan. Indeed, the Lord has made man with amazing capabilities (cf.

Psalm 8). The responsibility to act rightly – the measure of *true* freedom – is the charge man bears from his Creator.

Therefore, when reading scripture, encounter the living God who humbled Himself to join humanity in the Person of Jesus Christ. Indeed, enter into a greater union with the *Person* of Jesus Christ who loves each and every person in the world, for He has formed each according to His plan since before the beginning of time (cf. Jeremiah 1:5). Regarding the following poetry, please first read the selections of scripture from which the poems receive their names. Spend some time in prayer about the verse or verses, and then move to the poetry afterwards. The poems are not simply a commentary on scripture, though if it is the will of the Holy Spirit they might shed some light on the passages' meaning. Rather, they can be considered as elaborations formed from the scripture passages. The poems are not apart from scripture, but are testimony to the Word for His praise and glory forever more!

God the Father, embrace us as Your children.
God the Son, have mercy on us, sinners.
God the Holy Spirit, enflame our hearts with Your love.
And Blessed Mother Mary, carry us always to your Son.
Amen.

Exodus 3:14

The utterance of identity;
The statement of essence so simply spoken –
Not just a name but indeed
The secret of being itself:
"I AM WHO AM"
God speaks, and it is

Moses may have initially felt
Confused, even cheated at God's response
To his question –
Moses was human like us,
Expecting something more concrete
Than a statement about being

But there is not anything
More concrete than being!
God speaks the truth

In effect, although appearing
To tell Moses nothing specific,
God reveals Himself intimately
To this man – He shows through His word
The infinity of His existence,
He shows Jesus Christ, the Word, to a sinner

Contingency and necessity,
The finite and infinite,
United together in conversation

Unending Spirit, unending love:
Even though we pass away
From this earth and meet You
Face to face, You remain
As You always have been,
Ready to greet us anew –
Consistency, faithfulness

Trust in the Lord at all times!
He is literally always with us,
Walking the journey of life He has so
Graciously bestowed in us
By our side…
Every breath we take
We pronounce His name

Genesis 1:26-27

Over everything else in Your creation
You formed humanity in Your own image
And likeness, oh God,
Living Creator,
Loving Creator!

You crafted humanity from the dust,
From nothing we have been shaped
Like clay,
By Your hands

By Your Divine Mind You conceptualized
Two sexes, male and female,
A complementarity thus –
Inherently present in the giving and receiving
Of self…
You are present there in this
Deep union of soul and body:
The intimacy represents Your
Unfailing love,
Indeed Your essence

In this great existence, this great
Gift we call life,
Let us, oh Lord,
Never forget that You fashioned us
Out of nothing: *ex nihilo*…

That every human being
Has entered existence because of
A unique, beautiful, special
Thought of You, oh Lord,
Thought Itself

What can originate from this union
Your love gave to us, oh God?
As we are temples of Your Holy Spirit,
May we always maintain
By Your grace
A purity of mind and body

We who partake of Your
Love for us
Should give to You all we have,
For You have given us all You have
From before the beginning of time:
Your love

From this love our lives have
Their origin and end,
And with Your help
Goes forth the grace to live
With You in the future

This end is our origin,
And the origin our end –
All rooted in the Father's love

Genesis 15:5

Abraham looked up to the stars
As God had told him to do,
Gazing at the spheres of light
That speckled the black emptiness
Of space, the vast void
Of silence

How appropriate that God
Directed Abraham to marvel at
The stars, numbered as his offspring
Of the future generations

This vast expanse was viewed
Externally as a metaphor
For Abraham's interior capacity:
His soul, crafted
By God's own hands,
Was to be filled with His grace

The vast expanse mirrors
Abraham's docility to God's will,
The silence speaking so eloquently
The wisdom of the Divine

The covenant made with Abraham
God made to him as a total, complete gift:
Nothing was done to merit
This generosity in any way, save being
Open to the Lord's plan, His providence

As rain falls upon the earth
From which it came,
Abraham sought the living God
And was satisfied

1 John 4:14-15

I can call You by many names,
Many titles,
Lord Jesus:
Uncompromising Strength,
Hope for all nations,
The Blazing Fire of Justice,
Everlasting, Eternal Love

But even more intimately
I am able to call You
The Son of God,
Perfection incarnate
Of the Father

I am able to call You
My Savior, whom I can
Receive every day in the Eucharist –
The gradual sanctification You give me
So that I might accept Your
Salvation
In my own life!

How horrible it would be
If I knew of Your saving
Passion, death, and resurrection,
And yet did not embrace it!

I proclaim You as my Lord,
And do so from my heart –
But this is not enough to merit
Your kingdom,
But rather only the beginning
Of the journey to You

Speaking the Truth –
Yes, You are the Truth, oh Lord! –
Is indeed necessary:
Christ Jesus is Lord,
But I am called to *live* this reality
In my life,
And not only speak about it

Otherwise my personal profession
Of faith was mere words,
An empty sentiment
Without the works to join with them

Peter indeed professed Jesus
As the Messiah,
But our Lord did not call him
To stop there –
Peter eventually *died*
For Jesus,
Crucified upside down

This was the fulfillment
Of the words Peter spoke
Those years ago:
Philos love turned
To *agape*!

Let us always live for Christ,
Ready to profess with works
What we have known by faith –
So that the world may come to believe
That Jesus Christ is Lord,
And so that every person may recognize
That God dwells in him,
And he in God!

Psalm 44

With one voice
And one heart, we all
Sing the perpetual praise
Of the One, Triune God:

God the Father,
we praise Your holy name,
For You have given us
The most precious gift
Of existence!

God the Son, the Word,
We praise Your name, for through
Your Incarnation, we can relate
To You, the Lord God,
With an intense intimacy, and sacrifice
Our very lives
To You by the saving example
Of Your passion!

God the Holy Spirit,
We praise Your name, for You
Presented Yourself to us throughout
Salvation history, constantly
Renewing and purifying Your Church!

You, the Triune God,
Are the essence of generosity,
Of kindness and gentleness,
Of love,
The epitome of forgiveness and compassion –
You continue to give us unworthy recipients
Your love day after day

Receiving this love, we are ready
To succeed by Your grace in all that
We have set to do –
But now it seems that that grace
Has left us:
Have we done something to offend You, oh God?
Have You become angry with us?

Why, oh Lord, have we drifted
Away from You?
What have we done?
We were serving You justly,
Doing all things for You –
What have we done
To warrant this change in You?

Ah, My children, He says to us
Both individually and collectively,
I am God; I do not change –
This present suffering requires patience
And much endurance

It is thus – indeed, My will for you –
So as to make you stronger,
To build you up higher in Me,
In order to establish My kingdom
On earth to a fuller extent

So in a way, we receive His love
Even in the adversity of our lives –
We are united with Him more
Because we cannot find the consolation
Anywhere else

We cling to Him in hope
At all times – *especially* when
It is difficult, *especially* when
There is adversity through which
He calls us to persevere!

Forgive us, oh Lord, for when we
Have strayed from the docility
You have called us to have

Through docility we truly learn
What obedience radically means,
And through obedience to the Lord
We come to know intimately
The death He is calling each one of us
To experience personally –
A death to self

Do we live completely
For God yet?
Or does a part of us
Still need to be lifted up to Him,
Released from our hearts?

This does not take away
Any freedom we have or might have
In the future –
In fact, when we truly
Die to ourselves, the Lord
Exalts us beyond what
We could have had before,
And raises us to Himself!

Behold, the glory of God
Residing within each person of the world!
Behold, the love of God
Conquering the evils of the world
Through the charity we are inspired
To share by Him!

Our motivation, at that time
Of spiritual death,
Ought not be to receive
For ourselves a greater intimacy
With God – selfishness – but instead
So as to share it with all – selflessness

Indeed, we respond to the love of the Creator
With more love for Him,
Coming forth from the depths of our being –
We *love* Him,
And there are no other reasons

In fact, if we have ulterior motives
For wanting to die to ourselves,
Such as being recognized as holy by others,
That likewise is an area
In which we need to die to ourselves!

A constant process it is to die to ourselves

All is from God;
All is for God;
All then must be always
offered to God!

Psalm 51

Oh Lord, I am a broken individual,
Yearning for Your mercy –
I search the world for things
That could give me the equivalent
Happiness You provide,
But without the commitment
You require…
But I find nothing equal
To You there

I look within myself and see
Clearly for the first time
How sinful I really am,
But not with the shame
I used to feel –
The Devil's lies and deception
Are not as efficacious against me
As they once were

Cleanse me from my sins, oh God;
I desire never to offend You again!
The journey is long, tiring, and difficult,
But You are always at my side

For my life I praise Your name:
You did not have to grant it to me,
But out of love bestowed on me
The priceless gift of life,
And give Yourself in the Eucharist
To all as divine life!

My sins keep me humble, oh Lord,
And remind me of my human nature –
I am not You, oh God, nor want to be…
Let me ever fully be content
With who I am:
A sinner who yet is Your beloved,
Your delight!
This is something I have not earned;
Obviously, Lord, You know my ways,
Turning to sin when I do not want
To do so –
You have mercy when You
Are not obliged to have it, forgive when
It is not necessary to act thus,
And You do it out of love

Ah, what love You are, oh Lord!
What Love You truly are

Psalm 63:2-9

For You My Soul Is Thirsting

In every thought I think,
I long for You, the Truth;
In every word I speak,
I desire to praise You;
In every action I do,
I am seeking Your face

Even in the greatest sins, oh Lord,
I am searching for You,
Though I am weak and fall
Into worshipping false gods:
Lesser goods than You, oh Goodness

Can I honestly say that I desire You
Above all other things in my life right now?
Is it true that losing my soul
Profits me nothing,
Even if I gain the entire world
In the process?

Yes, I indeed believe it to be true

But is not by my believing it
That these things are true,
But because you, the Necessary Being,
Have to exist!

By Your Divine Mind have shown
Yourself to me over the course of my life

I thirst ever more for You,
Yearning to experience ever deeper
Your love for me!

What You will reveal to me in the future,
You only know –
Help me to remain open
To Your promptings, oh Lord,
So that I might be ready
To receive what You plan for me

I do not want to fail You!

By myself I can do nothing;
By Your grace all things are possible!

From all You have given me,
I long to be refreshed ever more
In the springs of Your love,
Being washed clean from my sins
In the waters of salvation

Just as water is necessary for survival,
Your love is to me now –
It was not always so in my mind,
But You are so patient and generous:
Let me never turn back
To the desert of my own making!

Your Love Is Better Than Life

If I had the choice of either
Dying and being with You, Love,
Or denying You and continuing to live,
Why would I even hesitate?
By Your grace I would seek the former;
By myself there resides ambiguity

Intellectually I understand why
I want to be with You:
You are God, perfect love,
And nothing happens at all
That is not somehow Your will

But there is more to be grasped,
More to be lived,
Than just an intellectual comprehension
Of Your love, and how it is
Truly better than life –
Something deeper is present that
Can be revealed if You so desire
For me to see it:
And You indeed desire that!

You hold me in existence:
Thus You show Yourself to me

And You want me to let You
Show Yourself to me,
But beautifully You will not
Force Yourself upon me;
You respect my freedom,
The free will You have given me

And so how fitting it is
That we return to the initial
Choice that many of the saints
Have experienced through martyrdom:
Because of my free will,
I have the capacity to testify freely
To You, oh Lord,
Even if that means my death!

But do I have the fortitude yet
To do so?

By You, oh Love so pure and simple,
I will have the strength if
That is my calling,
And spiritual martyrdom every day
Will be asked of all, again
By Your grace will it be perfected –
My life is in Your hands!

My Soul Clings to You

I am hungry, oh Lord,
And know that all the food of the world
Would not be able to satisfy
This hunger
Within my soul

I thirst, oh Lord,
And realize that all the water of the world
Would not be able to quench
This thirst
Within my soul

Only You, my God,
In Your body and blood,
Do I find the nourishment
For which I search,
The fulfillment which
I so deeply desire

And so thus I cling to You,
My Lord Jesus Christ,
Confident in Your power to work
Wonders not only in my life,
But in the life of every person
In the entire world!

The alternative frightens me:
To spend eternity divided from You
Because I did not cling to You enough!

To be permanently separated
From my true Love
Would be a suffering too horrible
To bear

But You, oh Lord, provide for me
The grace and salvation I seek:
Let me cling to You
Not simply out of fear of failing You,
But even more intimately,
Let me cling to You always
Because I love You,
Because I would do anything
To serve You

I cling to You because
You are the Creator,
And I am Your created

I cling to You because
You are the Lover,
And I am the beloved

I cling to You because
You are my Father,
And I am Your son

Ultimately there is nothing more
To realize from the heart
In this life than that!

Psalm 84

Holy Spirit, faithful Advocate,
Please enlighten my mind and
Enflame my heart,
Creating in Your time
The foundations of love within me,
So that I might be prepared
To enter Your house, oh Triune God,
When You call me to Yourself

Each person You created
Ex nihilo –
Oh, the magnificence of even
A single living cell! –
And call him or her back to You:
All things come from You,
And all will return to You, oh God!

If only people would accept
Their own mortality…
If only they would accept
That a moment with You
Transcends time itself,
That with You there is true peace,
The fulfillment of every desire
Of their hearts

Help me, oh Lord, to live this truth
In my own life,
For preaching Your most holy name
By my actions is more eloquent
Than the most precise oratory –
For indeed You guide
My steps day and night

Every person seeks happiness,
Seeks fulfillment;
You desire the same for them,
Oh Lord my God!
Even the most profound suffering
We can experience hides itself
From our reason,
For it, too, is a *grace* from God

Why?

Because by the adversity
We are united more intimately
With the passion of Christ,
Who experienced what we have suffered –
And so much more! –
Though undeserving of the pain
He bore for us

He did not merit the death we gave Him;
We do not merit the graces He gives us

But nevertheless that is the nature
Of the loving God
we so heartily praise:
selfless, self-sacrificial
Love!

Therefore, let me assert my unworthiness
Before You, Almighty God,
So that the emptiness
I display to You from within me
May actually be the preparation
You have willed to use
To fill me with Yourself
In Your time!

Psalm 95

To the living and perfect God
We sing together with joy
His praise:
The Unmoved Mover is constant,
Perpetually loving all His creation,
Calling each thing as it is,
Forming each by His own hands

Outside of time, He remains
Without change –
Though His universe may change
Around Him according to His will,
God does not alter in any way:
In fact, He dictates all
By His Divine Mind,
Orchestrating the great symphony
Of existence
In Himself

How can we approach such a perfect
Being as He?
How can we grow in intimacy
With Perfection when we ourselves
Are so far from it?
Far from Him!

God is omnipotent, yes, but also
Our humble shepherd, our guide –
He takes us by the hand,
Loving us to the end:
God loves His people, the sheep
Of His flock

But even though He has given
Himself to us,
We still retain our humanity,
That which by His permissive will
Is imperfect, sinful –
Fear not! His Mind conceptualizes
The greater good that will come
Even from a grave evil,
Comprehending it all
In the eternal present!

In God is found utter contentment,
Rest, peace, and joy –
By His grace let us not offend
This gracious God ever again,
But live our lives for Him, at all times,
Without condition,
Without hesitation!

Life is not long enough
To allow ourselves to make such excuses…

Psalm 128

Oh, the freedom that is gained,
The liberty that is realized,
When we turn from sin
And live our lives for Jesus Christ!

Prosperity is found thus,
The spirit thrives, delights
In our Lord –
If faced with either choosing Him
Or anything else, even the cumulative
Total of all of those things together,
Why would we even hesitate?

Why *do* we even hesitate?
The Lord is infinitely greater

He wants the best for us
Since before the beginning of time

He wants the best for us –
That which will not exclude great sacrifice

He wants the best for us
So that we can become like Him:
Self-sacrificial love,
Love itself

If we are to remain humble
And firm in our conviction
That Jesus Christ is Lord,
We must praise Him unceasingly,
Serve Him unceasingly,
Love Him unceasingly!

To do so brings a glimpse
Of heavenly peace into our hearts,
A foretaste of things to come
Loving the Lord means willing
The good for Him,
But He is Goodness itself, lacking nothing –
So a way to love the Lord,
In addition to loving the Eucharist
And Mary, His mother and ours,
Is to love others with *His* love,
Those who certainly lack much,
Who certainly need to grow –
In those too we see the face of Christ!

Marriage between a man and a woman
Is the representation on earth of the Trinity's
Unity in heaven, three in one –
That children come into the world
Demonstrates that this love
Is a love that creates,
Not destroys, that is open
To new life – the greatest gift of all! –
Not stifling the flame but embracing it

Let the flame – ah, the radiance of Christ –
Shine brightly forth
Into the world

Those that have an interior life
And recognize God's providence
In their lives share the living God
With everyone they meet,
Helping all to realize just how much
A joyful gift the Lord has given
By granting us life!

Peace flows through this act of love –
Where God is, peace is to reign forever,
For even the death of Christ
In its horrific violence
Sowed the seeds of a deeper peace to come
By the blood of the Lamb –
The peace of heaven

Psalm 143:1-11

Hurry to my help, oh Lord God,
The King of the universe,
For the Evil One attacks me
Again and again,
Ravishing my body and soul,
Weakening my will

I am not afraid of the Devil himself
Because I know You are infinitely
Stronger than he,
But I do fear the things he does to me,
Tempting me into sin – into discord,
Disharmony with You

A life of sin compared to a spotless death
Gives me a growing desire for the latter
Every time I ponder the choice:
Either A or B?
Is there a middle ground to be found between?

You want me not to only live,
But live well: with virtue!
By testifying to You through word and deed,
And renouncing the Evil One,
I am choosing in that moment
To live for a spotless death

But does that moment carry over
To the next instance of selection?
Have I responded to the grace in my life
From You, oh Lord,
To choose consistently what is divine
And perfect over anything else?

I cannot do this alone, my God –
It is not even that I feel lazy
And do not want to commit to You,
But instead that I do not possess the strength
To take on Satan alone:
I need You, oh Lord!

And I know that You will be there
With me every step of the journey,
For You are God!
Jesus, You experienced everything
I currently suffer, but without sinning
Even once…

Oh Great High Priest,
On my knees I crawl to You,
Begging for Your protection against the snares
Of the Evil One –
And through faith in You, the Son of God,
I can be sure that You will suffer with me,
And indeed have compassion
On me, a sinner

Revelation 11:17 – 12:12

The salvation of souls is not physically
Seen or observed by man,
But instead spiritually sensed,
Intuitively experienced,
Through prayer

We praise You, oh Lord, the Necessary Being,
Who has brought us out of darkness
Into Your light, which is gloriously
Light itself!

But we who see You must then
Serve only You,
For there will be many attacks
By the Accuser to prevent our serving You,
The One, True God –
The Accuser desires deeply for us to fall
Into his kingdom instead

The reward of living a good life,
Rooted in You, is not simply
The augmentation of life's quality
On earth, or reliving the best
Moments of our lives over and over again
In heaven –
Heaven is far beyond even our most
Comprehensive imagination of You,
The Perfect!

Heaven is gazing perpetually
At You, oh Lord,
The Lamb who was slain!

We indeed rejoice at such an immense
Happiness – that which is attainable
By living a life devoted to You
And nothing else:
Are we ready to make the commitment?

We should not love any person
More than our Lord and God,
Even family and friends –
Instead we are called to love
The person *God has made*,
The person *God has placed* in our lives,
The person that has the great capacity within
To glorify *His* name

Love each person according to
His or her identity –
And since we are all
Beloved sons and daughters
Of the One,
We should love each and every person
With a high, selfless love,
With the love of Him who has given
Us the precious gift of life

But God still comes first

But You have assumed Your power
And have begun Your reign;
The war has been won –
Now through You we fight
The remaining battles against the Evil One,
Confident in Your power, authority,
And most of all,
Your love

Romans 8:18-21

Are we slaves to sin in our lives?
Are there things that hold us down,
Preventing us from receiving fully
The Father's love?
Are we shackled by bonds
From the Evil One?

If not, let us praise without end
The living God for His generosity,
And be prepared to fight the Devil
In a different way,
Combating Him by the power of Christ –
Never fight alone, for alone
We fail in the battle against evil,
But with Christ we are victorious

If so, why are there those bonds within?
Have we believed the lies
That the Father of Lies has told us?
Even though it may not appear
To be so, receiving lies from the Liar
Is a suffering that eventually draws us
Closer to the cross of Jesus, for
Even sin is allowed by Him
For some greater good

The Devil's machinations work against himself,
For out of necessity, upon being attacked with lies,
We have to flee from him to Christ –
It is imperative

There is never any reason in our lives
To lose hope in Jesus Christ!
If we do so, the Lord would tell us
With the gentleness of a dove upon a branch,
To grow in our faith
So that we can trust Him further, love Him further
If we truly trust Him, there is nothing
That can shake us,
Nothing that can take us
From the Father's love!

The battle with the Evil One
Will indeed grow more difficult,
My brothers and sisters
In Christ Jesus!

There will be occasions in the future
When even the most appearing
In virtue and faith
Will fall into an abyss of despair
From which they themselves
Will not be able to leave –
They will need the grace of Christ,
But will pride prevent
Their receiving the Lord's gift?

The lowly will be exalted, therefore,
Those who have not been noticed
By the powerful, by the world,
But who have remained
Faithful to the Lord –
These chosen people, though imperfectly
Because of their humanity,
Have testified to God
In ways that even the best writers and orators
Have not yet been able to express:
It is the work
Of the Holy Spirit!

But again, we must repeat
To ourselves at every moment,
It is the Lord's will for us
To be tested:
It is His Church, and we are
Only the stewards!

If we believe this not only in our minds
But in our hearts as well –
Especially in our hearts! –
Then our faith will be surer
Than the things proven by the world

And thus we will be able, indeed ready
With joy filling our souls
With a song so sweet,
To cooperate
With the grace of God given to us,
The stewards,
So that the world may know
That Jesus Christ is Lord!

This is our goal,
My friends in Christ!
May the Father's will be done,
And may Jesus Christ
Be praised!

Part 2

Abandonment to God's Will

Since each person has been made in the image and likeness of God, man always has the capability to delve deep within himself to find the Living God present there. It is only a question of whether or not man will take the responsibility with which he has been charged and actualize this potential. If so, he acts in a fully human way, participating completely in the nature he has been given by his Creator. If so, he is living fully, and thus internally experiences peace and joy in his heart, even if suffering comes to him. The sufferings of this world are as nothing compared to the joys anticipated in Heaven.

The paradox, however, comes when man attempts to actualize this potentiality within him. Man cannot fully accomplish this important task himself, but rather open himself up further to the Triune God who loves him. Man can only take the steps necessary to be open to the grace of God, cooperating with it; God will fill him according to His time and will. But will man take the initiative to abandon himself to God? Both individually in the members of humanity and collectively as a whole, this opening of the heart and soul to God is the vital step to fulfillment in this life and preparation for the next, a *sine qua non* for the interior life.

Man is a relational being by his nature because indeed the Trinity is relational: as Father and Son give Their love to the Other with such perfection that an entirely new Person proceeds, the Holy Spirit (without being created, however), so does each person have the responsibility to share himself selflessly with others, and ultimately, with God. Since man is relational by his nature, he will indeed give himself to things in his life. The distinction is made, though, regarding exactly *in which things* he will invest himself. If it is not God that man seeks, he certainly will pursue other things that, in his mind, will substitute for the vast emptiness he feels inside of him from turning his back on the Lord.

Money, pleasure, fame, and the like all offer themselves to man as potential absolutes to which man can give himself fully. But when the glamorous shine of the world's allurements ceases to be, and the luster of these "things" is no longer attractive, those who have given themselves to these things have nothing left, and are even less satisfied than before selling themselves to the world. In order to prevent this downward spiral in the future, into which sadly many have fallen, man must take the responsibility with which he has been charged – that is, living in accord with his dignity as a person capable of experiencing God in his life – and give all he has to that same God who loves him with His entire essence.

What God creates is good; thus, the things of the world are *good*. But they are not God. Created things can never replace the Creator, referring not only to God but to man as well, for man, too, creates many good things in line with the plan of his Creator. Indeed, God Himself called man *very good*. Man, therefore, is called to emulate the Lord in selfless giving of himself.

God the Father, embrace us as Your children.
God the Son, have mercy on us, sinners.
God the Holy Spirit, enflame our hearts with Your love.
And Blessed Mother Mary, carry us always to your Son.

Amen.

Abandonment to the Will of God

Painful in the process, indeed, but lo!
The fruit this surrender bears
In God's time, according to the will
Of the Almighty One
When we abandon ourselves
To Him

Why does pain inflict us thus?
Is it from some thorn
From our past?
Or a current adversity plaguing
Our progress to the Divine?
Or even worries about the future,
About that which will come?
Namely, what God surely knows
But that we do not?

Abandonment to God's will
Is given as a gift,
Is received with a heart at peace,
Received with a sigh:
We let go of our own breath
And what we gain, thus,
Is silence.
Silence and Peace

Eternal Stillness,
Everlasting Tranquility –
Why, oh why, my brothers and sisters?
Why do we resist so strongly
The power of God?

It is because we are human:
Imperfect and sinful, and yet still
Made in His image and likeness –
He has made us "little less than a god"
Oh, the responsibility therefore
Not to waste such a precious
Gift!

Without God, we die and return
To the dust…
We have no strength except in Him!
Cooperation with His grace
Is needed for the journey –
The fulfillment of our nature
Is living for God

To encounter Him within
And share Him with the world:
Conversion, Evangelization –
Love

In Christ Jesus we find the fullness
Of life, of love –
He wants to give us that life,
That love!

Always, forever, without an end
Is His love for us –
All that is required of us
Is to fall into His arms
And surrender our lives to Him.
Amen!

Cast into the Fire

"You must not serve
Both God and mammon" –
Oh Lord, what words You say!
I am serving You,
Having paid the price,
Having suffered the pain

"Ah, my son, wait a moment
In the stillness
Listen to my Word come
To you in the silence
Let it penetrate your soul
With its everlasting peace"

Cast into the fire, the blaze
Consumes me from within!
The love of God moves me so,
Drives me to the precipice
Leads me to the edge
Of my existence…
What more is there to desire than this?

Out of my hands, without the control
I once knew well
I am shown the path to holiness
But on the way the sights so gruesome
And disturbing I witness passively

All the mammon of my heart
Being consumed by His love,
I am becoming free, but painfully

How far I have walked away
From the love I have sought
With all my heart – from Love itself!
How far I have wandered

Looking for sustenance
Where I knew none existed
Oh Lord, how patient and pure
Your love truly is! Why do You show me
Your identity thus?

My son, I ask you to be
Silent
I have shown you My love,
My essence
By keeping you alive –
By maintaining your existence

Cast into the fire, My son,
Your mammon no longer has a hold
On your heart
Only I remain!

"My God, my Lord!" I cried
In the most perfect adoration
I, imperfect, could ever but know
For a short moment, come and gone

Terrified of the Glory, unworthy
To look upon this Face
In the Eucharist
And yet finding myself walking
To receive the living God,
I remember that it is not
I who first loved Him,
But He who first loved me

Cast into the fire for the sake
Of our souls' purification:
The suffering is only
Temporary…
Eternity awaits!

Dying to Ourselves

In order to experience fully
The Holy Spirit in our lives,
Working without ceasing,
We must die to ourselves
To allow Him to move us
As efficacious vessels

This verb used – *must* –
Is intentionally utilized
Implicitly by the Saints' examples:
This issue concerns not only the spiritual life
But life as a whole,
Not permitting any room
For compromises with the Lord

It is not only "recommended"
That we die to ourselves,
Or only "suggested" –
It is necessary, imperative,
A *sine qua non*
For gaining true freedom
In Jesus Christ!

Is this a process that will require
Effort and struggle?
Will it be painful at times?

To both of these questions we look
To the cross of Jesus
For our answer:
Surely *He* exemplified
What this process is to accomplish

Is this a painful process?
Surely!
Is this a time of suffering?
Without a doubt.
So then why should I
Subject myself to this horror
When the world perpetually invites me
To invest in its pleasures?

It is because human beings
Have been created *to love*,
And this love is not
In order to take, but instead
To give!
The deepest love is self-sacrifice

Therefore, there is nothing
Fun or enjoyable, in the moment,
When enduring the growing pains
Of kenosis, but upon being brought up
From the depths of the soul by the Lord,
Upon completion, love is the product!
Indeed, God is love – always!

Receiving the Gift of Nothingness

In an act of preparation,
The Lord can choose to give
Quite the mysterious gift:
The receiver suffers by His grace
When granted the beautiful gift
Of nothingness

This internal solitude with God,
Not emptiness,
Fills the receiver with
A purifying darkness –
Where is the Lord?
Has He left me?

But the receiver of this nothingness
Somehow understands *by the peace*
And even the joy within him that
This fluctuation in the spiritual life
Is indeed from God, and not the Enemy –
And so he bears the cross with patience,
Waiting with endurance to have
This gift bear its fruit
From the Lord

With every gift there are immediate,
Proximate, and remote goods
Leading the receiver to the ultimate good
That is God Himself

The Devil will attack the spiritually gifted, however,
Attempting to convince the receiver
Who has acquired this nothingness
That no good can come from this purifying darkness

Immediately, the good given by God
Is a disruption of the receiver's normal routine,
A paradigm shift –
This disruption does not cause anxiety
In of itself, for God cannot sow anything
Against His nature that gives love, peace, and joy

No, this disruption guides the receiver
Into contemplation:
Mediation on his life and the way he leads it,
On his possessions, relationships, and priorities –
Perhaps he does feel a bit anxious
(a response to His God-given conscience),
Which is a wonderful result:
God is speaking to him thus,
Telling him to increase his fervor
And approach Him, the Lord, more readily

The receiver of this beautiful gift
Of nothingness now has a choice to make:
To either follow the Lord
With even more dedication or to continue
Living as he has been –
It should be noted that the Lord
Will not give this gift to one
Who is not yet ready…

In other words, the receiver
Of this bestowment of nothingness
Has already been seeking the Lord
Through prayer and supplication,
And *even still* feels anxious when considering
The ways he has yet to die to himself

The Lord would not usually give
The gift of nothingness to someone
Without a prayer life already firmly established
Because it would have no benefit;
The person would be even more repelled
From the spiritual life than before…

After the time of disruption,
If the receiver does indeed choose
To move forward, there is the great realization
That the Lord is a loving Father,
And that the gift of nothingness
That the Father has bestowed has shown the receiver
That he is insignificant in comparison to the God
Of incomprehensible glory –
He has grown in humility by
Receiving the purifying grace within

And so from this type of spiritual death,
The Lord paves the way within him
For greater things to come

These greater things would not
Have been possible without this
Time of preparation –
After experiencing nothingness
Intimately within him,
The receiver is a vessel for the Lord

This vessel has been washed
In the merciful waters of God,
Ready to hold the grace
With which the Lord
Will fill the lowly vessel
For the world's sanctification

The Mystical Union

Climbing the spiritual mountain
To reach the almighty God
Is done by digging downwards:
Uprooting within ourselves the weeds
Growing in the soul, by His grace
Finding purity anew –
Ah, but the intimacy with the Other
Experienced thus!

He prompts this journey, He sends
Forth His Spirit of life
To strengthen and guide us
To Himself – but where
Can I find You, oh Lord?
I know not how to enter myself,
How can I come to see
Your face?

It is when man realizes that the Lord
Dwells within him
That he becomes fully alive –
Gloria Dei Homo Vivens
Are we living at this very moment
For His glory or our own?

This intimacy with God is found
In the depths of silence, at the core
Of simplicity

God is perfectly simple…
When I stop "doing" things
To try to find Him, and instead do nothing
But simply *be* with Him,
I find Him in the passivity,
This peace of spirit and soul!
God *is* Being, Goodness, Love:
He holds all together in Himself

This passivity is necessary
In the spiritual life;
Will our eyes grow weary
From gazing upon His face
Within us? Never.
Not physically do we do this, but spiritually –
Done without action,
For we simply *are*
And He thus reveals Himself in the stillness

Never abandoned, never forgotten:
We are always in the mind
Of God – the Divine Mind!
Oh Lord, I seek Your face
By resting; I strive to live
By dying!

The mystical union between God
And man is in the silence,
In which the fullness of eloquence
Is most clearly expressed,
Most clearly vocalized

How beautiful it is that the
Eternal word of God
Speaks to the heart in silence!

When we listen with our hearts
And not our ears, what sweet
Music we hear within!
Hearts beating as one, uniting together
As one voice singing the praise
Of the almighty, ever-living God,
We live and die by His will,
in His time

Union with Him brings happiness
Beyond compare, and joy experienced within
Where God Himself dwells
Is the summit of spirituality –
This joy is deeper than emotion:
It is the very gift of God!

The Relationship Beyond All Others

If I am to live completely for God,
There requires the sacrifice of self
To invest in Him:
To sublimate my own desires,
Even those of my future,
In order to give myself
Totally to Him,
In the relationship beyond all others

With this conformed newness to God,
I am content with the prospect
Of suffering for Him
In any way He wills,
Even if the life I once lived
Is no longer possible –
This is what is necessary
In the relationship beyond all others

If every person in the world looks at me
With distaste, anger, and jealousy
Because of this relationship with God,
Their contempt rooted in sin I once knew
And still know at times,
There still remains a deep peace within me
Despite the suffering
Because the Lord has already chosen me
In the relationship beyond all others

If every human relationship I have or will have
Would be an adversity physically, emotionally,
Mentally, or spiritually for me
For the sake of His Gospel,
Let it be done!

I am willing to suffer that way –
Because all those relationships are still
Contingent upon
The relationship beyond all others:
If I am to love only Him,
And see this Love take my own love
And transform it to others,
Pouring a part of myself that was not
There at the beginning, but
Is now beyond my normal capacity,
His grace will have overshadowed me

I no longer live,
But only He
In the relationship beyond all others

And thus will every relationship
I have be one of joy,
For although suffering may come,
The Lord is the first and last –
And each relationship will shine
His grace not by my own light
But by His most perfect radiance
In the relationship beyond all others!

Part 3

God the King, We the Servants

If reading sacred scripture is the gateway to journeying deeper in the spiritual life, and upon experiencing that relationship grow fervently with the Lord, by the Lord, through abandonment to His grace and providence, the next step in the spiritual life is to recognize that His will for each of us is for our happiness. He desires to provide for us the fulfillment of our nature, that is, to love and be loved: to reciprocate the Father's love, self-gift for self-gift, and share this love with all. Therefore, we are the stewards of His plan in the world – God has given us all, as human beings, the potential to cooperate with His grace and bring His love to those who have never realized His embrace before.

This is a beautiful responsibility that each person has been given; it is not only for a select group of people, but rather the duty of humanity collectively and individually in its members to go into the world sharing the truth about man himself: that he is a being worthy of dignity, that his aspirations and hopes transcend the time period in which he finds himself but instead point directly to God, and that the battles he faces in his life allude to a greater cosmological war between the forces of good and evil. To declare anything less than these truths is an offense not against one group of people, but against humanity. Even if one does not believe in these spiritual realities, there nevertheless remains the responsibility for Christians everywhere to preach the Gospel to that person – and indeed to the entire world! – so that the individual might come to experience the light of Christ within his or her mind and soul.

Modernity calls for man to bend to its will of materialism and relativism: to belittle man to a tool in the larger infrastructural project of ideological solipsism, in which ultimately only the ideas of the current age are considered applicable, and only the issues of the current age are discussed with enthusiasm. Man must never be manipulated like this, not only because it attacks his dignity to transcend the world around him, but also, and indeed even more importantly, because he is not the highest being in the universe. Man has been made to be a servant of his Creator, the all-loving God. There is inherent dignity to be found in this office of service to God! There is charity to be directed to the Author of life out of love and freedom, not mindless duty and coercion. But even more profoundly and intimately, man's identity before God is not only found in servitude but also *in sonship*: a gift always to behold with gratitude and wonder!

The Lord has planned from before the creation of the world that He would love His creation and hold all of it in existence by that same love. He also elected to place man at a special perspective in the universe through the gift of his identity and his soul's rational faculties so that he might never forget his Creator and subdue the universe around him for the glory of that same Creator, whom he has the opportunity to call "Father." To casual observers this might seem to be only a metaphor for human love, as conditional and weak as it is. To hardened cynics this is only a futile human attempt to rationalize the horrible conditions of the world. But to a true servant of God, this is indeed the marriage of faith and reason that affirms and promulgates the sacred dignity and value of man.

God the Father, embrace us as Your children.
God the Son, have mercy on us, sinners.
God the Holy Spirit, enflame our hearts with Your love.
And Blessed Mother Mary, carry us always to your Son.

Amen.

Cooperation with Grace

If God willed for the salvation
Of many souls to be possible
By bestowing grace on an inanimate object,
Such as a chair,
He could do so –
He is God!

Perhaps this chair would be
A historical religious article
That would, for instance,
Levitate periodically or emit a bright light
On occasion –
If this be in the holy plan
Of the Father,
It would surely happen,
For all things are possible for God

Perhaps many souls, upon seeing
This special chair, should return
To the Lord when realizing
That He is the only explanation
For this unique phenomenon:
The object does not have
Such capacities *in se…*

Let God's will be done, then,
And His plan be accomplished
However He desires

But we human beings
Have been made in the image
And likeness of God!
Surely we, by our very nature,
Are much higher than a chair
That we ourselves have constructed

God has desired that we have
Dominion over the earth
And its creatures while still
Recognizing our own created nature;
We cannot escape the *comforting* fact
That we have been created by God

And thus, how much indeed
He can accomplish through us,
Who have the capacity to cooperate
With His grace, and who also
Have gifts and talents
Given by the Lord from our birth:
These two sets of abilities work together
For the building of God's kingdom!

The chair has no obligation
To do anything but simply
Be a chair,
And obviously there are no
Moral implications for any
Deficiencies

If the chair breaks, it is disappointing
Because of its historical and religious
Significance, but the chair
Will not be sent to hell because of it

But we, on the other hand,
Have been given so much by God!
We are indeed three levels above the chair
In the hierarchy of being:
Above the chair, or rocks, or sand
As inanimate objects,
Above the plants and vegetation,
And above the animals as well,
For the Lord has given us an intellect and will,
Those which set us above every other
Creature or thing on earth

We are thus called rational beings –
This gift gives us the responsibility
To cooperate with the grace of God,
And praise His name at all times!

If we do not use our intellect
But become immersed in our bodily urges,
We are no better, in a way,
Than the animals;
If we do not use our will either,
We are not living
As the Lord God has intended –
We are called to live for Him,
Using all He has given for His glory

We are still nothing, regardless
Of the many abilities we possess,
But with God and cooperation
With His will,
Countless souls can indeed be won
For Jesus Christ,
Because Jesus is the Person acting
Within us –
We can be vessels for Him

We have been given much from the Lord,
And to those who have been given much,
Much will be asked:
And yes, unlike the chair, plants, and animals,
We will be held accountable for how
We act in this world –
There will be judgment

But there is no reason to fear!
Live for God,
Live for others,
And there is nothing then
About which to worry,
Nothing around which
Our anxieties can revolve
Because of the immense Love
Lord Jesus Christ has for us all!

My God, My Love, My All

In Your body and blood,
Oh Lord my God,
I find the fullness of life,
The only true happiness
I can ever have
In this world –
That which elevates my soul
Beyond anything I could ever
Experience by human means

I thank You from the bottom
Of my heart, oh Lord,
For Your gift of Yourself
In the Eucharist!

The nine choirs of angels
All adore Your majesty,
Oh Eucharistic Lord;
In the Mass we perceive
Heaven on earth,
But behind the veil
Of the most holy Sacrament –
Increase my faith and trust in You!

I thank You from the bottom
Of my heart, oh Lord,
For Your gift of Yourself
In the Eucharist!

Heighten my fidelity to You
By allowing me to choose freely to attend
Faithfully the holy Mass every day
Of my life –
Why would I want to do any differently?

I thank You from the bottom
Of my heart, oh Lord,
For Your gift of Yourself
In the Eucharist!

By loving You in the Eucharist,
That which is received into our very bodies
Each time we attend the Mass,
Our lives will be entirely transformed
By You,
So that we may meet You in heaven,
In Your time,
Having passed through the veil
To see You as You are!

I thank You from the bottom
Of my heart, oh Lord,
For Your gift of Yourself
In the Eucharist!

Oh God, my Love, my All,
You are Source of my life,
And the Object of my
Ultimate goal

If only the world could see You
In the Eucharist through faith,
And desire repentance authentically,
Without selfish motives,
And go to You, the Eucharistic Lord,
Jesus Christ,
With love and openness…

I thank You from the bottom
Of my heart, oh Lord,
For Your gift of Yourself
In the Eucharist!

I treasure in my heart
The love You have shown me,
Are showing me now,
And will show me for eternity –
Despite my failings,
You are always faithful,
Oh Lord, my God!

I thank You from the bottom
Of my heart, oh Lord,
For Your gift of Yourself
In the Eucharist!

Like the many saints before me,
I desire to follow You
Wherever You lead me

I thank You from the bottom
Of my heart, oh Lord,
For Your gift of Yourself
In the Eucharist!

Like the many saints before me,
I seek Your face at every moment,
Although sometimes erroneously
In lesser goods…
Nevertheless I return to Your
Eucharistic Light,
Perceiving thus the foretaste
Of the Light I will see forever,
By Your grace,
In heaven

I thank You from the bottom
Of my heart, oh Lord,
For Your gift of Yourself
In the Eucharist!

My God,
My Love,
My All:
I love You

I love You

May Your Name, oh Eucharistic Lord,
Be praised forever!
Amen.

Radix Animae, Anima Ardens

If God would ever stop
Thinking about us, we, contingent,
Would cease to exist:
He *has* to be, and there is nothing else
More to say

But what if we do not believe
That God exists?
Surely our great capacity for reason
Will be able to prove He exists –
After all, man is the highest being
To grace the earth with its presence…?

But we remember quickly that we ourselves
Have not always been –
When we ponder omniscience, it is a crime
To think that we can strive for this,
Or even come to grasp it
As a goal attained, an accomplishment:
As though the collective efforts
Of humanity can ever equal
God's perfection

Often we do not even understand
Ourselves –
The full depth of the human person
Is indeed a mystery to us,
Even though we participate fully in it!

Attempting to deny this fact
Will not make it disappear…
By extension, closing our eyes
Will not make the Creator of both
Eyes and sight
Cease to see everything about us!

The capacity humanity has been given,
The incredible gift of free will:
What a grace from God to choose Him
Freely, without coercion!

The Transcendentals of the Good, True,
And Beautiful:
These all allude to the glory of God;
Physically we cannot explain *why*
We perceive these things in part,
Even though we can discover *how*
We are attracted to them

The how versus the why…

But these transcendent concepts
Are nothing compared with the fulfillment
Of all of them at once,
God Himself!
Oh the Perfection of goodness, truth, and beauty,
We praise Your name!

And this Perfection has given us each
A living soul

At the root of this gift
Is His love for us,
Dwelling within us is His Spirit

Indeed, the root of all is God Himself

This gives us all an inherent dignity,
Having been created by Him, and in
His image and likeness!

If I limit my considerations
To only the physically observable,
Then there are only those things,
And nothing more…
Nothing more?

Upon death, then, do you feel
Content with your contingency?
Your life here on earth,
In proportion to the existence of the universe,
Is but a blink of a blink
Of an eye –
And to think that God
Has always existed and always will…

Just because we do not understand
This great mystery does not mean
That it is not true,
That it is not real,
That it has no bearing or influence
In a modern, scientific world

In fact, the realest entity of all,
The almighty God,
Shows us at all moments
More and more about ourselves –
Who He is, and who we are
In relation to Him

The moment we step back
And fathom His love for us,
And fail…
Is the moment we begin to understand!
Being able to drown in humility
Through this death to self
Sparks a flame to ignite our spirituality

This flame, ignited by God's love,
Continues by His love,
Burns ever brighter and hotter
Within us the more we recognize
That nothing will ever separate us
From this Love!

The instant we stop speculating
About what lies beyond, and instead look inward
At ourselves – and see God within! –
Is exactly when we find *everything*
We have sought for our entire lives:
We find the Lord dwelling there, loving us as His children!

The Gift of Free Will

God does not force Himself upon us,
Even though the Divine Mind knows well
That He is the best possible entity
We could ever receive
In our lives

It takes our free will to choose
From our own hearts
Whether or not to accept Him:
We freely walk to receive
Our Lord Jesus Christ in the Eucharist –
We ideally take each step toward
The living God with an interior freedom

"I am not worthy, Lord,
But Your will for me
Is to come to You, to develop
A deeper relationship with You"

Therefore I choose freely
To do exactly that for Your glory

Like a candle burning
With a soft glow of fire,
Penetrating the darkness around it,
So we choose to go to God
By our own choice –
Making us then higher than even the angels!

But the responsibility dwells
With us, then: are we ready
For such a challenge to call us forth
To action?

The more we accept this
Free will we have been given –
That which is not meant for license but
Living truly free! –
The more we realize how omnipotent
God really is

He can take our bad choices –
Our falls, failures, shortcomings,
And sins –
And use them for some greater good
Known but to Him

This is true omnipotence!
God did not make everything over-controlled
Where we as human beings do not have
Any power in making a decision,
But instead He works with this freedom,
All actions in accord with His Divine Mind

This is true *agape* love!
God loves us so much
That He would rather give us
The choice to either love Him
Or not to love Him

Knowing quite well that many will
Turn away from Him,
He still sacrifices Himself
For our salvation –
Once upon the tree,
And perpetually through accepting
Our denial of what is good, just, and ordered
For what is evil, unjust, and disordered

This self-sacrificial love is exemplified
Perfectly on the cross:
Jesus, God Himself, experiences
The effects of the gift He gave
To each one of us…
But frees us from our sins,
Rectifying the relationship between Him and us
Through His blood!

Trusting God

Trusting God the Father

From origin to end, our lives
Are but a single breath
And what lies between seems
Like a song beginning and ending
With only the first melody being played –
Cautiously, somberly, sadly we pass by
With this song of reality

Where is the hope that remains?

Where is the joy of life?
Oh God, where have You led me?
To move, to eat, to sleep –
Why is all this so?
These are the questions we have
To ask Him
Daily –
These are the questions of life

You were able to ask those questions
A moment ago because I love You,
The Father says…
You existed then and now because
I have intended it to be so:
Since before the
Beginning of time

Since before I constructed
The universe with My own hands,
I knew that you were to be
In existence
For a certain period of time –
Do you remember Job, my Son?

And then my eyes were opened
As if light had just passed through them
For the first time!
I knew, not only from my mind
But deeper within, from my heart,
That I have a loving Father

That I am called to trust
My Father;
That I need to trust
My Father

My life lies in His hands,
Yet for some reason I still wish
to see ahead – I stop:
do I desire to have the mind of God?

With a moment of silence
I answer myself with a 'no' –
All that I need in life is His love

And I receive this love
From my Father
By trusting Him

Trusting God the Son

You, the Beloved of the Father,
Are equal to Him, of the same
Essence and nature…
Humility at the center of this
Infinite love, beyond
Human comprehension that
Omnipotence takes on meekness
Transcending

The epitome of this Love,
Oh Jesus Christ,
Is a two-fold manifestation
Of Your divine plan…
Your divine plan:
That which You have known
With Your Father since before
The beginning of time

Two-fold is the manifestation
Of Yourself as the Son
To humanity:
The Incarnation and the
Paschal Mystery, my God!
That You would enter humanity
As one of us, and then die for us –
Love, ah what Love this is!

Although we cannot grasp this Love,
These two occurrences give an insight ever sweet
Into Your nature,
A gaze into the eyes
Of Eternity unlimited –
Into the gaze of human eyes as well

Oh, those eyes! Those eyes of Yours,
Lord Jesus,
Express a pain that I cannot
Quantify
But deeper still they show a Love
From Your heart, Your soul –
Salvation

Still, Lord, You are God:
Why are You upon that cross?
You are God – take Yourself down
From that murderous device
And show the world
Who You really are!
Please, Lord!
Please, Lord?

But without speaking a word
To me aloud, the Word
Communicates His purpose
By remaining there, dying there,
On the cross

Ah, those eyes! By looking into
That window I see not only
A human soul, free from sin,
But God divine, eternal and perfect!

By my sins I sent You to die there,
Jesus Christ my Lord:
I am truly sorry for all
My transgressions!
Every time I fall into sin
I crucify You again

Oh the agony I feel for You,
The righteous anger I bear
In my heart on Your behalf –
But gazing into Your eyes, ah, yes
I begin to understand what all
This chaos means

My soul is washed clean
In Your eyes of mercy,
Your heart ever sacred!
Mercy triumphs over revenge –
Grace abounds ever more

And so, oh Lord, I come to realize
That You are calling me
To trust You –
Not only with my mind
But also with my heart,
Especially with my heart!

For through trusting You,
You will transform my heart
To Yours, my life
To Yours –
Even until death

And I receive this love
From the Son
By trusting Him

Trusting the Holy Spirit

Every breath we take is another
Gift from God!
The Love between the Father
And the Son
Is You, Holy Spirit,
So strong, so beautiful –
Indeed, the essence of strength,
Of beauty!

How can I contain Your love,
Oh Holy Spirit, that You give
Not only to me but all
Of humanity unconditionally?

You send me forth to the world
Like a lamb among wolves,
But fear is not necessary

You guide me ever near
To Yourself by moving
Those who revere You to show me
The way

I find myself speaking far beyond
My own eloquence,
And writing beyond thinking

Words flow onto the page
Like a rushing river of peace!
Holy Spirit, those are clearly
Not my words alone! They were stirred
By You, Who are united perfectly
With the Word,
Jesus Christ!

Help us all to be open to Your promptings,
And let me never cease to praise Your name –
You dwell in Your Church:
Unite it,
Guide it,
Keep it from all harm:
Remain with us, Lord

We cannot do anything without
Your help, oh Holy Spirit,
Source of Wisdom

All things are possible
In You, by You,
And once we embrace this,
Let us do everything *for You*

And I receive this love
From the Holy Spirit
By trusting Him

Amen.

Part 4

Redemption from Sin in Christ

Perhaps no better can man recognize continuously that he is not the highest being in the universe than by realizing his own weakness and sinfulness. Not fundamentally is he flawed, for God has made each person in His image and likeness, but from an inherited tendency towards weakness and sin from our first parents who were faced with the same choice either to remain faithful to God or to disobey Him. Indeed, there was a *choice* involved, a microcosm of man's incredible gift of free will he has received from God. Today, too, man finds himself surrounded by choices to make, decisions that metaphysically reflect the transcendent foundation of morality. Times do change, but this reality man faces is immutable.

To one who is living in sin, upon rare personal reflection, he will view himself as relatively free from sin and living well because at that particular moment he lacks an honest perspective of his own behavior due to a lessened interior freedom and increased fear. On the contrary, to a saint engaging in the same internal reflection, of course at a deeper level than the person living in sin, he will see virtually every flaw and shortcoming he has committed at the forefront of his memory, and each painful recollection will carry the weight of sadness for having offended God even in the slightest way. Paradoxical as it might seem, the more growth in holiness is experienced by the generous gift of God's grace, the more one intensely recognizes that he has not earned anything the Lord has given him. Indeed, he knows intimately within him all of the reasons why the Lord should not have given him the particular graces accompanied with living for Him, due to the undeniable, reoccurring fact of sin. Humility before God and man, then, is the saint's response to the Lord's bounty: to proclaim to the world that the saints are by no means perfect testifies to the great capacity of man to be resilient in the journey towards God.

In the inexpressible beauty of God's perfection manifest in both pure justice and mercy, therefore, He became incarnate through the Person of Jesus Christ for the redemption of the world. The hope for man that Christ shows in this most mysteriously magnificent act of love reminds all that no matter what sin has been committed, the Lord is ready to take the burden of that darkness away: both in the historical act of the crucifixion, done once for all, and the continuous sacrifice of the Lamb in heaven. The former is accessible to human reason only by seeing a man innocent of any crime suffering greatly on the tree, whereas the latter is beyond the human capacity to know but through revelation man is enlightened of its beauty. Ultimately, how fitting it is that in the Sacrament of Reconciliation God's forgiveness is sent through a man, a priest, who in that great sacrament of healing and in all things is to be an eternal icon of Christ's cross. To account for one's sins does not admit defeat, but rather obtain Jesus' victory. Let us always be open to the Lord's embrace of healing, then, and have courage to walk with Him through temptation into the beautiful light of grace.

God the Father, embrace us as Your children.
God the Son, have mercy on us, sinners.
God the Holy Spirit, enflame our hearts with Your love.
And Blessed Mother Mary, carry us always to your Son.

Amen.

Despite Our Sinfulness, God loves

Too many lives have come and gone
Set in darkness, no hope of dawn
Our Original flaw
Our humanity seen

But in our lives there is nothing to fear
For God, in His mercy, is always near
Our strong Sustenance
Our Perseverance

When we ask *ourselves* where to go
We try but fail, *God's* grace will show
Our Confidence
Our Happiness

Our goal should be to gaze, tranquilly awed,
At the riches and wisdom and knowledge of God
Our sole Joy
Our true Peace

So we are imperfect, yesterday and today
But even still, with trust and faith, we say
We cannot
God can

Piercing Perfection on Man's Behalf

Both pierced for the sake of the good,
Though suffering did indeed occur thus –
Their hearts for the Father were punctured:
Our Lord's heart physically,
Our Mother's spiritually,
Both emotionally without a doubt at all

What solidarity there is present
In the hearts of both mother and son –
The Mother and the Son!
What glory, what humility to behold!

Mary spiritually speaks this
To her Son, the Divine,
And He lives it for her
In dying on the cross

I desire deeply to be ever conformed
To the Sacred Heart of Jesus
And the Immaculate Heart of Mary –
Both pierced by the permissive will
Of God the Father

Oh Lord, let my heart too
Be pierced with Your love,
And for the sake of Your love!

When pierced for the sake of the Gospel,
The wound my heart will receive thus
will not be detrimental
To my life, but on the contrary,
Be an internal fire consuming me,
Uniting me to my Lord Jesus Christ!

Tears of Love

Oh cleansing stream of reinvigoration
You provide for me, oh Lord,
My God!
These tears of love flow
Not from my eyes,
But from my soul,
Crying out with joy to You!

How I have failed You so many times,
And yet Your hand is upon me still,
Guiding me toward the Light,
To Yourself! –
The responsibility builds
Within me never to forget
Your mercy,
A task that is not a burden at all

My soul sobs tears of sorrow,
Tears of fear
At the thought of failing You
Again

My soul sobs tears of sorrow,
Tears of fear,
At the possibility of not using
The gifts You have bestowed upon me
To their greatest potential
For Your glory!

My soul sobs tears of sorrow,
Tears of fear,
At offending You by my sins
Even in the slightest anymore

But so much deeper than these anxieties,
These pains within me,
Is the Source of life
From which this river of tears flows
From my soul

Jesus Christ gives freely to us
An inherent dignity to suffering,
And truly by His sacrifice,
We are healed!

This makes my soul cry more
Than all the other reasons
Combined!

This gives me hope in Him,
To lay down my own life
In service to Him,
To die and be raised up
From the tears He so gently
Wipes away from my face

Do not cry, My son!
Rejoice, be glad,
Sing your love instead!

And to my amazement
When I look into Your eyes,
I see tears gliding down
Your cheeks –
Oh, the glistening window
To *that* Soul!

Those tears of love
From Love glide down Your face
Because You love me, oh Lord,
Because You died for me,
And all I can do in response
Is thank You from the bottom of my heart,
And thus live for You always!

My soul cries for Your love,
Tears flowing forth from within me
Like a dam having burst –
And You so totally provide
That Love
I desperately seek,
Turning Your tears
Into blood shed for me,
For all!

To Drink from the Stream of Life

Grace and mercy flow, the inundation of my soul,
From the source of this Divine stream:
From the side of Christ,
His sacred heart pierced,
Comes forth eternal salvation

Water and blood together flow
From the precious body of our Lord

And behold, He gives His blood
To satiate the deepest yearnings
Of our hearts:
The fullness of life with Him!

Oh, let me quench my thirst
By drinking of this saving source of life!
Let me approach You on my knees,
Absorbing Your love internally

Your eyes pierce my soul
With the same intensity as Your heart was pierced
By the soldier's lance,
Having had my aggression purified,
And only peace remain by Your grace

Oh let my heart be nourished
With Your love, Jesus, all my days!

Parched and dry, my heart cracks
At the deprivation of my life
Through the terrible effects of sin –
Oh wash me, Lord, in Your blood,
And water the ground of my souls
Through *our tears together*

So that in Your time, oh God,
The harvest of my soul might gather
The fruits that You have grown
Within me, for Your people

Part 5

Unity to the Cross through Adversity

This same Cross on which every person, through his or her sin, placed the Savior of the world for His death has become, paradoxically fitting, the hope of all in times of adversity by Christ's own blood. One cannot even begin to comprehend the suffering that the Lord endured for the sake of humanity; the adversity He faced for man's salvation indeed provides for every person a demanding example that is literally impossible to follow by man's efforts alone. Man is too weak, but in hope the Lord is merciful and helps each carry his cross. The Lord becomes for us what Simon of Cyrene was for Him.

If Jesus Christ had not died on the cross, wounded excruciatingly on behalf of man, there would be no reason to accept the truth of suffering's dignity. If there is not any redemptive, unitive value in suffering that brings the sufferer closer to God, then there would be no reason to suffer at all, no reason to bear the cross for the Lord in order to grow in holiness. The world in which man finds himself today is increasingly opposed to the possibility of suffering in society. But the *telos* of society's quest to eliminate suffering is misdirected. The goal today appears to be to eliminate all suffering from the world, which is indeed impossible. The very fact that man, in his fallen state, is capable of sin means that there will be discord, violence, and self-destruction that will inevitably lead to suffering. This is allowed by God in His permissive will; often we do not know why He permits things to happen that appear contrary to the common good. But in the trust we have through faith in God, we are able to accept more easily that God allows suffering and evil in the world *so that greater goods can come* in His time and according to His will. Although this is quite challenging to receive emotionally and psychologically because we are not in control of the situation at large, God's grace and mercy gradually permeate our souls if we accept His love for us; by this internal sanctification we become more docile to the will of God. God wants only the best for His children!

How beautifully fitting it is that God, in His plan of wisdom, would choose to save man from his terrible fate of doom and death by sending His only Son, Jesus Christ, to take the sufferings of the world onto His shoulders. To some this may seem too good to be true, and thus impossible – after all, how could God ever care about human beings who constantly disobey Him anyway? *God is eternally merciful*, and loves His creation with everything: this love indeed extends to the point of self-sacrifice for the sake of man's redemption. Man, then, is called to respond with gratitude to God for the gift of life

He has given to each person: a gift granted not according to an individual's merits before God, but rather to all people equally. Salvation established, man must move forward by the Lord's grace for his continued sanctification, that which will be attained, with God's help, through the marriage of faith and good works.

Suffering, when it indeed comes, is a way for the afflicted one to demonstrate how much he loves the Lord by patiently enduring the cross, and remaining obedient to God the Father. It is not humiliating or dehumanizing to suffer; instead, as Jesus Christ became man and suffered to the point of death, suffering is an instance in life at which man is fully human, fully alive.

God the Father, embrace us as Your children.
God the Son, have mercy on us, sinners.
God the Holy Spirit, enflame our hearts with Your love.
And Blessed Mother Mary, carry us always to your Son.

Amen.

My Own Cross To Bear

When I look at my Savior
Upon the cross, suffering
Overwhelms my soul
Because suffering overwhelms Him

I tell Him that I am sorry,
Deeply sorry, beyond the capability
Of the expression of words, I am sorry
Because I put Him there…
By my sins and transgressions,
And by the sins of all humanity,
He is displayed there, dying –
Dying such a miserable death

Oh, Lord, let me enter into
Your crucifixion with You –
Let me participate in that which
I, not You, have earned!
Let me ease Your pain: sacrifice
Me instead! I should be
Punished

"Ah, my son," He says to me
From the cross looking down
Upon me, with Love flowing
From His eyes,
Flowing from His hands
And side!

Love tells me that I
Can participate in His suffering –
By bearing with patience and love
My own cross
For Him

The cross I bear is nothing
Compared to Yours, oh Lord –
Is this said in humility?
"I know," He says to me, "This is
The cross I must bear,
The cup I must drink
On my own"

"And you do suffer much,"
He tells me; Love says to me
That He is proud of me
And I feel His embrace
From His outstretched arms
On the tree!

For the first time in my life,
I have nothing at all,
And yet possess all

For the first time in my life,
I see nothing through the tears
I shed for Him,
And yet gaze into the depths
Of wisdom and grace

Lord, please provide in my life
The humility and obedience
To bear my own cross
For you – willingly
And with all courage

Emulating You is my goal
And Eternity with You
Is my prize –
That which I do not deserve at all,
But that which You are willing to give me
By Your blood

The Sufferings of This World

It is said that the wrath of God comes
When He lets us experience the consequences
Of our actions…
Well, He must do that quite often,
Looking at how broken the world really is

But He does so out of love!
He is love!

Humanity brings on itself
The suffering it endures, for God
Does not want us to suffer
In His active will; He may allow
Suffering to take place so that
Some greater good,
Known to Him alone,
Could come about in His time

But why, oh Lord, do You let the suffering
Overwhelm us so?

I do not let it overwhelm you, My children,
He says to us,
With love pouring forth into our hearts –
I love you all and want
What is best for you

You will find the best, the thing you seek
Most above all else,
In Me…

Suffering entered the world through sin,
When Adam and Eve chose to sin and therefore
Disobey God's plan for them:
When humanity increases in sin,
The suffering experienced collectively is magnified,
And thus no member is exempt from enduring
Some type of affliction

How is it, then, that the God
Of the entire universe
Came to save us from this fate
In the Person of Jesus Christ?
After all, we do deserve the punishment
For our crimes against the Almighty!

Through taking on the sins
Of the world, Jesus bore
The punishment for us when He died
On the tree

Salvation: that which we do not even begin
To merit in any way,
But that which we receive with solemn
And joyful hearts,
As an act of generous, self-sacrificial love
From Love Itself

Once, for all, sin and death
Were conquered, and by Christ's
Passion, Death, and Resurrection
We have gained eternal life with Him –
Now the responsibility falls on us
Not to waste this enormous gift!

We have faith in Jesus Christ;
We hope in Jesus Christ;
We love Jesus Christ!

Let our dedication to You
Never cease, oh Lord –
Both in the easy times to profess Your name
And in the difficult times:
Especially in the latter, Lord!

And so if You, Lord Jesus, will for me
To experience suffering in my life
So that I may grow closer to You,
So be it!

I say this not because I know
That this is what I should say,
But because You are transforming
My heart to Yours,
My life to Yours –
All in Your time

With this growth in You,
It is even easy to let go of myself: freedom!

After all, knowing the other options
Offered by the world and the Enemy,
There is now no ambiguity in my heart!

You freely chose to give me life, oh God,
And thus I choose freely to return
My life to You in service –
Both are done out of love! –
For indeed my heart is overflowing
With joy divinely inspired

The Weight of God's Gifts

Why, oh Lord, have You given me
Such gifts that I have not earned?
I do not have what You have perfectly,
Namely, holiness

And although I walk the path
Toward that beautiful end,
I am only beginning the journey

And yet You have inundated me
With Your grace, with so much
That I feel overwhelmed, even
Sorrowful at times...

For I know
That I will not be a proper
Steward of the talents
You have so graciously bestowed:
will they accumulate any interest at all?

What You give is never a *heavy* burden,
For Your yoke is easy, Your burden light

But by receiving what I have received from You,
I do enter into greater solidarity
With Your precious cross,
Deeper union with the Word
Made flesh

I feel isolated, abandoned by those
Who once walked with me;
Their endurance outlasted my expectations,
But yet they now cease accompanying me
On the journey…
Will hope cease as well?

I look into Your eyes
And already know the answer!
For with You is found rest and peace,
Oh God, the Good Shepherd!

My fears no longer hold me
In their suffocating grip;
They are subdued by the Lord
Like a strong breeze blowing
The leaves of a tree

Silently falling,
Resting softly on the ground,
Forgotten by man
But not by God

Let me never look back, oh Lord,
But instead follow only You
And go where You tell me –
It was, is, and will be
Not from my own strength
To carry this cross, this weight
Of Your gifts

But You will ask to carry me
And my cross for me,
Out of love,
And oh Lord, let me have the humility
To assent to that offer,
To let You bear my sins
On Your back,
To let myself fall into Your arms
Of love!

Part 6

Simplicity, The Song of Heaven

There is a harmony that flows from stillness, and a joy that originates in tranquility. There is music that comes from silence, and clarity that emanates from inner reflection. *In* all these qualities of peace, and *through* all these qualities of peace, God is present, speaking to the soul with the eloquence of quietness. Man has been given by the Lord the capacity to hear Him encouraging his soul with love – in the ceasing of movement and sound, God beckons the soul to venture out of itself into union with Him. Will man respond with a generous heart? Will he heed the call of the Lord?

God never forces or coerces man to follow Him. Instead, He respects the gift of free will He has bestowed in the heart of man, and simply extends to man the invitation to deeper union with Him, the invitation to exactly that which man himself seeks but often does not recognize: his own quest for happiness and fulfillment. He frequently does not directly ponder the origin and end of his goal, both of which are God Himself, but nevertheless has profound spiritual movements within him every day as he moves forward in his search for God. Ultimately, since the Lord only extends His hand towards man in respect of his personal freedom and dignity, man must reach out and grasp the divine – the assent of interior union – in order that his fears and doubts would be subjugated to the growing peace and tranquility he finds in God.

But will man reach his hand to God, calling for support lest he fall into the abyss? Will man possess the humility to ask for help? These are questions that are only answerable on an individual basis, for although man collectively walks generally in a certain direction, for better or worse, only the individual person can say for himself whether or not he will rely on God for everything he has. The essence of this disposition of humility is found in simplicity. This simplicity is a foretaste of what Heaven will be: the perpetual gazing at the Triune God, the outpouring of eternal love.

Man's simplicity is shown to some extent in his contingency, for if God would take away his breath, he would die (see Psalm 104, Job 34). It is also reflected in man's dependency on others for care and support. But man himself, adhering to his fundamental simplicity if he so chooses, becomes an icon of the Holy Trinity in Christ, for God is eternally, perfectly *simple*.

Knowing and accepting man's inherent simplicity can be profoundly insightful in how to follow God. Indeed, it is a powerful reminder about how to live if one desires to be truly happy. Why, then, do we all fall into the temptation of making our lives so complex and busy? It is because in everything we do, we see a good to be obtained or produced: God creates and it is good, for He is Goodness itself (see Genesis 1). We naturally will feel attracted to His creation because of its goodness and beauty, but God's creation is not God Himself, of course. We must choose between God and everything else when deciding whom to worship – will we worship God or will we worship the things of this world? We know intellectually that we should choose God in this situation, for many reasons. The will must follow the intellect, however, and so it is not enough merely *to say* we seek God, but actually seek Him in reality.

In the end, what man can think, say, and do has the potential of being incredibly complex, for God has given man a powerful mind. But that is not *who he is*. Man is simple, in the image and likeness of God; all else man possesses is meant as instruments he can use for the Lord.

In these following poems from Part 6, there is the opportunity for you, the reader, to place yourself intentionally in the position of the first-person narrator of the poems; through prayer and discernment you can find the peace for which every person searches each day by accepting God's great love for you in a deeper way. These poems in particular can be considered as a set of conversations with God the Father that you yourself can have, if you choose. Let the Holy Spirit guide you, so that you might be set ablaze in a new way by the Love between the Father and the Son. May Jesus Christ be praised forever.

God the Father, embrace us as Your children.

God the Son, have mercy on us, sinners.

God the Holy Spirit, enflame our hearts with Your love.

And Blessed Mother Mary, carry us always to your Son.

Amen.

Longing To Have the Heart of a Child

I anticipate the love of the Father
Like a young child waiting
To see his parents
After a day of work

I seek the love of the Father
Like a young child desiring
To see his parents smile at him
When they walk through the door,
And, content as ever,
Mutually giving the gift to each other

I embrace the love of the Father
Like a young child hugging his parents
Upon seeing them, his eyes full
Of joy and excitement

I am content by the love
Of the Father,
Like a young child feeling secure
At night after his parents
Tuck him in bed,
Not feeling anxiety in the slightest

Father, my God, You supply me
With all of these amazing experiences
Each and every day

All that is required of me
Is to live not as an equal to You,
As a father like You are,
But where my identity truly lies:
As one of Your beloved sons

All that is required of me
Is to give myself to Your loving care,
And let go of the tendency
Towards self-reliance

All that is required of me
Is to love
As You love

Steeper yet
These callings grow,
More difficult
These duties seem

But with God
There is no reason to fear:
He embraces us
With Love, and guides us
To do the same –
All is from Him,
And all is for Him

Loving Those Who Hate Us

I find in my life
I consider no person an enemy

It is natural to have a few people
With whom it is difficult
At times to coexist,
But this normal fact of life
Does not make those children of God
My enemies

Yes, I consider no *person*
In my life,
Past, present, and God-willing
The future as well,
To be an enemy

But I still have one
Enemy that will perpetually
Fight me: evil

The Devil and his minions
Are indeed enemies of mine,
Enemies of all people,
But they have no power over me,
For Jesus Christ fights my battles
For me now

This was not always so
Directly in my life –
Of course the Lord extended
The invitation of liberation,
And I accepted this
On an intellectual level

But somewhere inside I still
Considered myself strong
Enough to fight the Evil One alone,
Only asking the Lord for help
From the mind but not
The heart as well

Now I realize how dangerous –
And indeed ineffective! –
This strategy was!

Now I cling to the Lord
With everything I have,
My soul crying out,
As a babe, for the protection
From the Enemy I so deeply and
Desperately desire

And from this genuine,
Humble petition,
I let the Lord work,
And He does so

Demons literally flee in fear
Even at simply uttering
the Most Holy Name of *Jesus*!

If there are people in our lives
Who hate us,
We are called to love them
Even more –
We bring Jesus Christ
To them by giving
Them Love Itself

But we cannot love the Evil One
And his fallen angels,
Now forever demons –
They already had their opportunity
To serve the Lord,
And chose, once for all,
To reject Him

We always have the chance
To improve, to repent;
The forces of evil are
Doomed forever, separated permanently
From God, but we can return as children *daily*!
I pray fervently, oh Lord,
For forgiveness if anyone in the world
Considers me an enemy
Because of something wrong
I did to him or her that caused
Pain to flow, attack, destroy…

I desired deeply the exact opposite,
But perhaps I did not bring You,
Jesus Christ,
To that person in a time of need,
Disrupting the harmony
We had together:
Between the person and me,
And between You and me

If this be true,
Oh Lord of mercy, forgive me!
Let Your child be healed,
And let peace reign once more

Let Your love shine upon us all,
Oh Lord, Your majesty and splendor
Filling all Your creation with a sweetness
Of the spirit:
Let Your peace reign on earth!

By himself man cannot sow lasting peace
Because of his fallen nature,
But with You, there is mercy and forgiveness,
From which true peace will inundate the world
With the grace of the Holy Spirit

The Humanity of the Priesthood

The Lord personally chose by name
Twelve men to follow Him –
Twelve individuals who, like all people,
Were imperfect:
Who were sinners…

They left everything to follow Him,
Not knowing where that decision
Would lead them

If they did know at the time
That the choice they made to follow
That Man would eventually bring them
To their deaths as martyrs for Him,
They would have at least hesitated,
Perhaps even refused

But the Lord had the entire plan
Of His Church
In mind when He selected them

Jesus today still is calling men
To the Holy Priesthood,
The institution that the Lord Himself
Established,
And that the Lord Himself
Renews

In persona Christi:
In His Person should the priest
Die to himself and act
In the Lord, by His grace

The priest, like Mary, lets the Lord
Overshadow him,
Therefore purchasing by the blood of Christ
The glory resplendent
Of *sacerdos in aeternum*,
One day at a time

Does he deserve such a gift
To be bestowed on him forever?
Does he merit the indelible mark
On his very soul?

To both of these questions
The negative must be given honestly,
For the priest too is a sinner
Seeking the Lord's mercy,
Clinging with all his strength
To the salvation Christ provides

But sometimes the priest forgets
His supernatural calling
And strays from the Person
Who gave it to him –
Sometimes the priest commits sins
Which surprise even the most hardened
Of sinners

Because of the grace the priest receives,
He is indeed held to a higher moral standard,
And when he does not meet this level,
There is much tumult and suffering

Lord, please forgive every priest
When he has sinned against You
In large and small ways;
Lord, please heal all those
Who have been wounded
By a priest, in large and small ways;
Let Your mercy and love
Embrace them all: the priests and the people!

But nevertheless, despite the grave sins
Priests have committed throughout
The history of the Church,
The priesthood of Jesus Christ prevails!
Christ Himself is the perfection of the calling,
Taking upon Himself the exemplification of the
Supernatural vocation
Through the blood of the Cross

Would that every priest in the world,
From the newly ordained to the young at heart,
Be ever conformed to the Sacred Heart
Of Jesus Christ,
And live his life according to the sacrifice
Of the Lamb –
Not without his own faults,
But with the hope that comes from God

The Music of the Soul

Christ is the conductor,
The Church in her vitality
Is the orchestra:
And through the Sacraments we receive
Such beautiful music
To fill our souls

Harmony and peace strike a chord
Together
In this cosmic symphony

But lo, there appears some dissonance
Beginning to disrupt
The music within each person;
When we fall into sin, the harmony
Once established within us by Christ
Slightly wanes – we are indeed
The stewards of this music,
Imperfect vessels for this perfect melody

But even though we might not
Provide the spotless environment
To hold such sweet a refrain
As Christ Himself in the
Eucharist,
He still conducts the symphony,
The Church still plays it out!

Though unworthy even to hear
The heavenly chorus, we nonetheless
Return
Asking for mercy
And receive the music for our souls
Again

In doing so, by clinging to Christ,
The great Maestro,
We find the strength by His grace
To maintain this dramatic opera
Of suffering, death, and
New life in Him!

The Soul's Security

When night turns to day
As the sun shines its rays
To crush the darkness
Like shattering stone,
My soul is lifted up by Him –
A clearer sense of things
Even at the end of slumber

Comes a heightened perception of reality
Upon waking from sleep,
Upon resuming the journey started
Long ago

Sleep finished, the senses fully engage –
And awake now, ready to live
Another day: but for what?
Is the journey itself the absolute
Of life?

For whom will we live this new day?
For ourselves?
For God?
The choice is there;
We must choose one or the other;
There is nothing in between

This choice is absolute, without
Any ambiguity in its nature

Either we will live for ourselves
Or for God, but beautifully manifest
Is the generosity of God:
When we choose Him, our humanity
Is brought to fulfillment, exemplified
In Christ Jesus, fully divine
And yet fully human

There is a security in the truth
Given by the Truth Itself:
That which we have not
Earned or merited by our own effort,
But instead is freely bestowed on us
From God

Let us rest in this gift,
Safe in mind, body, and spirit
From all that can harm us –
Let us learn to trust in Him,
And thus begin to share
His mercy with all

The Willow Tree

I picture Your love to me, to all,
Like the branches of a willow tree,
Oh God –
The branches still fall to the ground
Even after the winds bombard them

So, too, Your love to humanity,
That which You have made
From Your own hands,
Comes even after the gales
Of sin threaten
To blow us all away

Is it too much to ask why
This mystery is, oh Lord?
Is it not proper to inquire
The nature of Your ways?
Do I not possess the ability
To understand all You have told me,
Tell me now, and will tell me
In the future?

Ah, My son, listen to Me now:
I love You, indeed unconditionally,
And like the branches of the willow
My love is soft, gentle, caressing –
You are a beloved son
Of My own heart

And I call on you to be patient,
To be persistent in your vigil
Awaiting My will for you

But why, oh Lord, do You call me Your son?
Surely I do not deserve this;
I will try to obey, but will do
Even better if I but know the reason *why*...
If I but know the reason why?

Conditionality is not true freedom,
For it gives implicitly
A hypothetical situation
In which free assent is still possible,
And yet not from the depths
Of the heart's selfless love

My son, you have much to learn,
Much room for growth –
And this is a beautiful thing!
Remember that I AM,
That I made you:
Your failures do not have the final word
Because I love you: I AM the Word

I AM the Lord, and you are indeed
My son, a human being
Created in My image and likeness,
Not a machine without the capacity
To love

The desire to understand
Is a gift from Me,
But you would not understand
What, how, and why I act
Even if I told you directly,
Even if I showed you but a glimpse
Of My Divine Mind

I did not create you
To be able to understand
Those things fully,
But only parts of them
And only occasionally

Do not be ashamed,
But rejoice in your humanity
With your weaknesses
And your imperfections!
They are what make you human,
What makes you My son…
I AM the Creator,
And you are the created, you are beautiful

And so finally these words have brought me
An intense, palpable peace,
Realizing for the first time how
To understand fully:
The foundation of the heart
Leads the mind to grasp
Myself, the world, and even
The Lord to a certain small degree…

But without the heart's openness
To God, the mind
Lies dormant, its pursuits
Next to nothing

If the willow tree lacks the roots
It so desperately needs not only
For stability but also to acquire
Nutrients from the earth,
It will wither, die,
And fall to the ground –
Likewise we will fall
Into the darkness, into the void
If we do not have our hearts
Constantly fixed on Jesus Christ!

But do not be afraid!
"With the Lord there is found mercy,
And fullness of redemption" –
If we come to know, love, and serve
The Almighty God here in this life,
We will be with Him forever
In the next!

The willow tree's beauty
Lies in its simple transparency,
For its branches move *with* the wind,
Its gracefulness dependent on even
the slightest breeze
To initiate the daily dance of flow

Let us, too, brothers and sisters
In the Risen Lord Jesus Christ,
Be ready to be moved like the willow
Internally by His most Holy Spirit
So that we may be able to testify
Externally to His power and glory,
Confident as never before
In our identity as beloved
Sons and daughters of the Father

Part 7

Perseverance to the Father

To support or oppose something is not dependent exclusively on speaking accordingly, but often is demonstrated also through action. Society may not explicitly say that it seeks worldly things more than God, but by its collective actions one can easily decipher the truth. In this environment it can be rather challenging to have the perseverance necessary in the spiritual life to meet the Lord upon death and gain access to eternal life. After all, this commitment takes a lifetime, and in a world that is wary to commit to anything, regardless of duration, modernity frequently turns away from this noble task of pursuing eternal life with God, dismissing it as a foolish quest and a waste of life's opportunities for pleasure.

To be immersed in this culture of emptiness and self-inflicted pain is draining, and the first way the Evil One attacks is by clouding man's perception of God's infinite love. If man succumbs to this attack, hope slowly ebbs away, leaving man without footing on his climb up the mountain towards the summit where God Himself dwells. But God remains with him despite the Evil One's deceptions; in fact, it is in the Lord's plan in the first place to have the Evil One present in the world at all. To have freedom means to have the potential of making a choice, and to be responsible when doing it. The Lord gives man a choice between Him and the world, between the ultimate good and lesser goods. It is truly that simple.

Man is not isolated when climbing the mountain of his life to God, for not only can man experience the Lord on the journey through prayer and introspection, but also through each person of the world as part of the Body of Jesus Christ. In God's infinite wisdom, He established the Church through the Person of Jesus, and this Church continues today and will continue until the end of time. Indeed, the deepest longings of the human person consist of the desire for belonging – to love and be loved by all. There exists in the heart of each person the yearning to be embraced not for what he or she is able to do, but for who he or she *is* – a child of God. From this foundation upon which true society is built, an ethos founded not on taking for oneself but *giving of oneself*, man can persevere to God the Father in hope.

The stakes are indeed high when contemplating the true meaning of the human person and whether or not each is participating fully in his nature by living for God in holiness.   To fathom the incredible gravity of the sanctification of even one person! How much joy all must share together at the prospect of helping a brother or sister reach the gates of heaven! How much pain all must bear together at the thought, God forbid, that a brother or sister has forever chosen the wrong path and no one opened his mouth in constructive protest in order to help him or her see the light of hope in God. Truly, the battle for man's soul continues to be fought, but there is no reason to fear – *Christ* is the perpetual hope of man.

God the Father, embrace us as Your children.
God the Son, have mercy on us, sinners.
God the Holy Spirit, enflame our hearts with Your love.
And Blessed Mother Mary, carry us always to your Son.

Amen.

No Turning Back

When we accept You, Lord Jesus,
For the Person You truly are,
Namely, the Son of God
And our Savior,
We are only beginning the road
To union with You,
Only starting the journey
With You

We then have the opportunity
Either to live our *entire* lives
For You,
Or to not do so –
Which route will we choose to embrace?

It may not be that explicitly shown
To us in our lives, having an unambiguous chance
To embrace the Lord or not:
Many battles of the spiritual life
Are instead fought in the daily routine,
The daily grind as it were

Daily life – the habit, the procedure,
The schedule we have had for weeks,
Months, years,
Even decades

But the apparent monotony
Does not detract from the importance
Of taking each thought and action
Captive for Jesus Christ:
In fact, the importance
Of living for Him *heightens*!

The Evil One attacks regularly
By making us feel complacent,
Feeding us the comforts and securities
Of a daily routine so that
We forget the true glory of God,
Resplendent and beautiful!

We are called, however, to use
Our daily lives as a testament
To persistent hopefulness
In our Lord!

Remember always, my brothers and sisters
In Christ Jesus,
That the Devil is not able to attack
Efficaciously someone who
Does even the simplest, most mundane
Tasks with a deep love
For God and neighbor

This is the heart of charity:
To serve, in great or small ways,
With great love,
Without counting the cost

If every person consciously performed
One act a day with such a selfless
Disposition directed to God
Like this,
Imagine what a surplus of grain
From the harvest of humanity
Would come forth thus!

The grain is peace;
We are the soil;
The harvester is Christ

Are we ready?

And so with an ever stronger
Conviction within me,
I cling to the Lord
And humbly beg Him to protect me
From ever turning back again!

The life we all live
Is much too short even to hesitate
Slightly in the quest
To live our lives totally for
Jesus Christ our Lord!

We need not be anxious;
We need not feel rushed –
These are the seeds of the Enemy…
Anxiety sows discord,
And no peace is found there

But a calm urgency to preach
The most holy name
Of Jesus
Is truly that for which
The world so desperately thirsts

Prince of Peace,
Please prepare our hearts
For Your harvest so that
We might be fertile ground
Upon which the wheat of justice
May grow, and the grain of peace on earth
May come to provide lasting food
For the entire world's sanctification:
In Your time,
And according to Your will!

The Essence of Holiness:
The Perfection of Charity

This universal calling from the Lord
Penetrates our hearts, speaking to us
From within the deepest caverns
Of the soul

If the destination has already been placed
On our hearts to have us found worthy
To reach the ultimate Destination,
We ask ourselves how to walk the road
That will lead us there

This road has many paths divergent
From the straight, correct way –
Many narrow trails seem to deviate
From the main course

Is this intended, meant to be?

Indeed, as many as there are people
On this earth,
There are corresponding paths to holiness
That eventually bring souls
To arrive at the face of God

And He sees all of them
At all times, forever

Holiness is not *exclusively* piety,
Although piety surely can lead a person
To holiness if the expressions
Of prayer are genuine

The Pharisees were considered pious
By the Jews because they
Strictly adhered to the Law,
But were they justified before God
By their *holiness*?

When we pray in a pious fashion,
We must examine the reason
Why we do so –
Discerning honestly the motivation
Behind our actions

Are we acting piously
Totally for the Lord
And His glory,
Or instead in order to fill ourselves
By doing so? Or is it a mix of both motives?

If our piety is indeed for God's glory,
Let Jesus Christ be praised!
Continue doing so with the full
Spiritual appreciation
That it is the Lord
Whom we praise,
Not ourselves

If our piety rather is to some extent for ourselves,
It becomes something to discern deeper,
Something to give to the Lord
Freely,
Out of humility,
Out of love for Him
And not ourselves

When we enter into the dwelling place
Of God within us,
We find that the exterior signs of prayer
Are dependent on the interior disposition
We have received from the Lord –
All is from Him,
And all is for Him!

Let *His* name be forever praised!

And so holiness does not originate
In what we do,
But in who we are as beloved
Sons and daughters of the living God!

Holiness does not even end
In what we do,
But in *retaining* our dignity
As beloved sons and daughters
Of the living God! Our actions
For God will come from this
Inherent dignity retained

How do we preserve this disposition, then?

Charity comes from this disposition
Because the Lord is working through us,
As He is indeed love!
True holiness, living the life
Of a saint of God,
Is to know how sinful we really are
And nevertheless act for others,
And not ourselves!

This comes from God,
Who desires to give charity to us,
If we are but open to Him –
Let us live for God, then,
With hearts burning with *His love*
That we can then share with all
Whom we meet,
Each and every day of our lives!

The Journey

Out of Darkness

Human beings we are,
Not human "doings" –
We exist: at the core it truly is
As simple as that

But we know we have not
Always been:
We have come into being
Not of our own power,
And will leave this world the same way

Contingency

God is not like humanity in this way:
We are blessed to say He made us
Like Himself – a profound gift,
An eternal joy!
But God has always been, is,
And will be forever more

Necessity

Once we have accepted this mystery
Not from our minds alone but also
From our hearts, our core,
We are led by Him beyond…

Guided by His hand
Out of darkness into the light
Of Truth:
Oh, indeed behold the blinding light!

Into Truth

Coming into the Truth,
Jesus Christ Himself,
We find hope, peace,
And love beyond
All measure, beyond
All comprehension –
Something not earned or deserved,
But given as a gift of love from Love Itself

And yet Christ, beyond all comprehension, still
Humbles Himself to the end –
He gives His life to us
In the Eucharist –
To receive Jesus truly present,
Truly there
In the Blessed Sacrament!

How do we know this reality
With any amount of certainty?
Not only because Jesus said so –
"This is My body" –
This *is* My body, He says!
But also from pondering the very nature
Of the Triune God

We find the Truth there as well:
He is *agape* love –
Sacrificing Himself perpetually
For us, who, though unworthy,
Dare to approach the
Altar of Sacrifice

We walk by faith
And not by sight:
We walk toward the Way,
The Truth, and the Life –
And receive Him
In Love!

Sent Forth

Entering into Communion
With the living God
Gives us a responsibility – a duty, a charge! –
Given by Love Itself

We are sent on a mission to preach
The Name above all others –
Ah, the freedom experienced,
The peace realized within!

Truly, the equilibrium of the soul
Is maintained again and again
By His body and blood!

Not to keep inside myself, however,
But to be shared –
The gift of love
From Love Itself

This Love must be given
To all attending Mass,
To every person in the world –
"Whom shall I send?" He asks:
Love desires to send His people forth

Oh, Lord, I am unworthy
Of receiving such a calling,
To be a priest for You –
But I undoubtedly feel Your promptings
And after receiving You as the Truth,
Shining against the darkness,
I do not hesitate, and say with the confidence
Found in Christ Jesus,
*"Here I am,
Send me!"*

Time's Steady March:
The Heartbeat of God

Despite all perceptions to the contrary,
Humanity is always moving forward:
we cannot stop this progression,
This steady, uninterrupted march
Of Time, the measure of change

We live in the Present,
Having each passing moment
Drift in silence into the Past,
Approaching each reality
Yet to be seen,
Yet to be *lived*,
In the Future

Present constantly becoming the Past,
And Future the Present –
The steady, uninterrupted march
Of Time, the measure of change:
Nothing can disrupt its cadence

But You, oh Lord, never change
And so are outside of Time,
Outside of this reality
That appears to control us
By its inevitability…

But it cannot control You,
For it is Your tool,
And You its Master

You, Almighty God, see all of Time
In the eternal Present;
You experience all that has been,
Is, and will be
Right now

And yet I find myself drifting away
From Time's steady march,
And rest in the stillness of Eternity –
I know not how! –
But what I discover There
Is beyond anything found within Time's rhythm

God's heartbeat radiates forth
The very conceptualization
Of Time!

The Unmoved Mover dictates
Himself the cadence on which
Time marches, telling contingent creation
The mode of change to experience
Without changing Himself

And how I have perceived this,
Again I have but a clue:
Serenity and Tranquility Incarnate,
The resounding drum cadence

Indeed, behold: the drum of Time,
Is the heartbeat of the Most
Sacred Heart of Jesus!

How precious, how perfect,
How loving You are,
Oh Lord our God,
With the essence of constancy
Enveloped in Your beauty!

To Seek and To Find

Every person has etched on his heart
The desire to seek and find
The meaning of life;
How beautiful it is that God,
Who planted that desire from the beginning,
Sought and found us first

The Son of God, the Word,
Speaks to humanity from His Heart
To our hearts

Comprehendible are His words
And yet transcendent in meaning,
They gently pierce the soul

From before time began the will of God
Is told in the present – and man
Listens intently

"What do you seek?" He intimately asks
Each person listening – without
Audible words He inquires the health
Of their souls, though already knowing the answer!

Oh, the responses He receives
From those who do not know,
And from those who think they know!

We all are seeking our origin
And our final destination – the same
Search, the same quest:
Christ is the Alpha and the Omega,
The beginning and the end

What else is there further
To seek?
What else is there further
To find?
In God alone are our souls at rest

Two Steps Forward, One Step Back

I want to be a Saint, oh Lord,
Living my life completely for You –
But it seems as if my momentum
Is prevented by something
I cannot fully understand:
When I make spiritual progress,
Sin pushes me back

Does my humanity get in the way?
Does it inhibit my spiritual growth?
Do I need to change who I am
In order to reach You?

Is there a difference between
Who I am and
What I do?

Ah, My son, I formed you
In the womb, and have made you
And each member of humanity
Little less than a god –
Do not think you are invincible
Or a failure, for indeed
Both are lies from the Enemy!

Virtue is found
In between extremes

My son, cease speaking to Me at this moment
And listen instead:
I am the Word!
Patience with My plan is what
You need at the current moment…

I AM the One to make You holy,
And I AM the One to transform your sins
Into greater goods,
But you have to let Me do so first

Growth in the spiritual life
Is slow and difficult,
But the Lord has the entirety
Of entirety
In His gaze at all times –
He has a plan!

What is necessary for us
Is to grow more docile to His plan
Of love for us –
To die to ourselves even in our desire
To grow in holiness
By our own efforts alone,
And let Him take us along the path
He has made us to take

When this liberation occurs, we rejoice! –
Because we will have realized
Where our identity truly lies:
We all are beloved children of God!

It is not what we do that defines us,
But who we are…

Thus, we move forward with hearts
Pouring out love for the Father,
Confident in His plan for us,
Ready to live for the purpose, the mission
For which He has formed us
From the beginning
To embrace in our lives

Part 8

Gloria Dei in Caelis

What glory awaits every person upon his death if he remains close to the Lord, for the light from Light Itself will permeate his soul for all eternity, and he will see God as He is. This is the hope with which man is called to live each day, the peace with which he is able to persevere. Indeed, the sacred truth of the human person lies in God Himself, the origin and end of the human condition. Separating man from his Maker only serves to isolate him from true fulfillment: it is not a matter of popular belief, that is, that it is only valid to adhere to such beliefs if a certain number of people share the same convictions. The truth of the virtuous person's final resting place, rather, does indeed transcend the factions and divisions that man has tried to make in the world. God ultimately sees past the walls man has erected and thus sees man himself, as he is. When God looks at humanity, He sees His sons and daughters in Christ Jesus. Ultimately, the Lord has charged man with the responsibility to prepare himself for leaving the created world after a time, and return to Him, the Father.

It is logical to believe, *ceteris paribus*, that with the perception of virtues and vices with which every person succeeds and struggles in this life, an individual would be called after death to give an account before God of his or her life's deeds. Faith illumines man with Truth that is beyond his mind's rationality, but also confirms what his reason can determine alone: what is called Judgment surely will come upon every human being according to the will of God. This initial meeting with God after death to give an account of how well we have lived our lives will be both incredibly intimidating and amazingly comforting: God's justice will ask much of our souls for virtue, but at the same time, God's mercy will set our hearts at ease, permeating us with perfect, enveloping love. It is at that moment that a person realizes with the greatest profundity yet that he or she is a beloved son or daughter of God, and the Judgment to be received from Him is true, for He is Truth.

After this account of our lives has been given, God will render the verdict of judgment, and we will either be sent to heaven, hell, or purgatory. Heaven and hell are permanent judgments, while purgatory is temporary, serving as a state of purification for souls so that after a time of chastisement, they can enter as well into the beautiful Beatific Vision for eternity. Needless to say, the stakes are high for each person, and while the salvation of Christ through His blood has saved all from damnation, God still respects the freedom of man. If man does not choose God freely, God will not force Himself upon him.

Indeed, it is not enough only to state one's belief in the Triune God, but to live with the same conviction on a daily basis.

Man possesses neither the power nor the authority to change God's plan for judgment that will surely come to him; every person finds death approaching at some point. Declaring atheistically the non-existence of God does not make judgment irrelevant, for a created being could not affect in any way the power of God the Creator by a mere statement of arrogance. Man should not be afraid of his lack of power before God, however, but instead should be content with what God has given to him.

Beautifully, this truth extends to the Cross as well: even at the point of death, Christ *remained* omnipotent, and won for man the chance to live with Him forever. Eternity with the Lord is that for which our souls long; living for God is the portal through which this goal can be realized. May Jesus Christ be praised!

God the Father, embrace us as Your children.
God the Son, have mercy on us, sinners.
God the Holy Spirit, enflame our hearts with Your love.
And Blessed Mother Mary, carry us always to your Son.
Amen.

The Love of Jesus Christ

Our lives are too precious not to love,
Our hearts too pure not to joyfully sing
For the Lord Jesus Christ has made us thus
And so let on high His praises ring

He is the image of the invisible God
And yet too so tied to our lives:
God Himself walks upon the earth in this Lord Jesus
And we can follow Him if our heart so strives

Why singular for "heart", why not plural?
Does not each one of us have his own?
True as this may be, in Him we are one
For on the cross this is perfectly shown

Are we to understand this great mystery?
Do we have the capacity to know God thus?
Are we strong enough to endure His suffering
And love Him as He loved us?

The truth is, without Him we are nothing:
Insignificant, weak, and bare…
But "in Him who strengthens me I can do all things"
If I but give myself up to His care

And so when we all feel angry or sorrowful
Filled with rage or full of tears
Let us always be mindful of His *loving* sacrifice
That alleviates all anxieties and fears

The Perpetual Sacrifice

If you do not enjoy attending
The holy sacrifice of the Mass,
You will certainly not enjoy Heaven:
There you will find not
A reliving of the best times on earth,
Or peace and tranquility
Without cognition remaining

No, instead you will experience,
God-willing,
The perpetual sacrifice of the Lamb
Who was slain for us,
Jesus Christ our Lord!

This eternal sacrifice is all
We ever need in this world,
All we will ever desire
Upon reaching Heaven's glory

For by then our lives
Will have been conformed to the Lamb,
Living among the wolves
Of our days on earth;
Purified from our failures,
We will see God in the face!

Am I a lamb or a wolf, oh Lord?

Only the saints can enter Heaven –
Both those canonized by the Church
And those known but to God
As having merited such a reward!

The only thing stopping us
From gaining this as well
Is that we do not fully want it!
We do not yet desire to give ourselves
To our Father

Fear not! It is not how we have begun,
Or even how we are now,
But how the status of our souls is
At the end of our lives,
When the Lord calls us home
To Himself…

Learn to love the Mass,
Dear brothers and sisters
In the Lamb who was slain!
It is literally Heaven on earth –
Why would I not want
To go and receive God
Into my body and soul?

Examine your lives honestly,
And the Lord will show you
The things preventing a deeper
Intimacy with this holy
Sacrifice of the Mass

Be patient!
Be vigilant!
Be saints of Jesus Christ!

The time will indeed come
Quicker than we anticipate
When we will see the
Heavenly sacrifice,
And by our choices
It will be determined
Whether we enter into the Glory
Or remain outside
The gates forever…

The Rose of Fire

Ardently burning but not consumed,
An icon of the Bush
That spoke to Moses the Divine truth;
The sweet fragrance of grace pours forth
From Your immaculate heart:
Mary, our Most Holy Mother

A blossom of red light
Among the thorns and sufferings of the world,
Docility surpassing humanity's limits –
Inspired by God's gracious love…
A rose without thorns but nevertheless
Her own heart pierced
By the thorn of a sword:
Mary, our Most Holy Mother

Ad Jesum per Eam Ipsam,
Interceding from glory on high,
To bring us to the heights
She herself experienced within her own womb
And experiences now forevermore
In the Beatific Vision, at the side of her Son:
Mary, our Most Holy Mother

If we say from the depths of our hearts
That we trust in the Lord Jesus,
We then receive His sweet grace and mercy,
Encouraged by Mary, our Most Holy Mother

Ah, this Woman most pure, most radiant
Who was chosen first to receive
The fullness of grace, bountifully overflowing:
Mary, our Most Holy Mother

We joyfully sing to God Almighty
With the melody Mary herself sang
In her most blessed *Magnificat* –
We look together at God in Heaven,
With her holding our hand all the way:
Mary, our Most Holy Mother

Sedes sapientiae,
You bore the living God in your womb,
Gaining an intimacy with God beyond
That of any other person in history –
A foretaste within you of heaven to come:
Mary, our Most Holy Mother

This rose, our advocate, shines
Ever brightly to the world –
In the loving embrace of this rose,
We are shielded from the turmoil
Of the world,
From the machinations
Of the Evil One:
Brought to Jesus in her mantle,
Covered safely by her petals:
Mary, our Most Holy Mother

Enflamed by the Spirit,
You became for us the New Eve,
The singular vessel of grace,
Queen of Peace,
Queen of Heaven!
Mary, our Most Holy Mother

Ignorance of you is to disregard
Our calling to be truly human –
You had the choice to accept
Your most blessed vocation;
Coerced or forced you were not…
And you said yes freely to God,
Mary, our Most Holy Mother!

This is the Woman, the Rose of Fire,
Whom we are called to emulate
In our lives!
Mary, our Most Holy Mother,
Ora pro nobis
Peccatoribus,
Nunc et in hora mortis nostrae.
Amen.

Mary, our Most Holy Mother,
We love you and go to you
As your children,
Forever and always meeting the Lord
Through your guidance,
Through your love!

To Grasp at Utter Perfection

Upon reaching the depths of fulfillment,
Relying solely on the grace of God,
Nothing else in the world seems to matter –
When everything comes to cease
From His gaze of perfect love

To become a Saint is not as challenging as it may seem!
By our *own efforts alone*, we see every obstacle,
Every wall – and fail!
Until that point of brilliant illumination
When everything comes to cease
From His gaze of perfect love

To recognize Him thus is but the beginning,
For we are called to receive all the more
That ever-perfect light of goodness,
Indeed, Light Itself! –
When everything comes to cease
From His gaze of perfect love

To become a Saint is not as challenging as it may seem!
Mind illuminated, heart set ablaze, eyes opened anew
By the Almighty and Ever-living God,
We fall into the Arms of peace forever
And trust completely His plan for our future
When everything comes to cease
From His gaze of perfect love

So that we might see the Light,
See the Lord – Him Whom we have put to death!
To see Christ humbled, and yet exalted!
And thus in Him to share the faith with every soul
By clarity ignited
When everything comes to cease
From His gaze of perfect love

To become a Saint is not as challenging as it may seem:
Abandonment to His will, constancy in fidelity
And a burning love for His sacred heart
– Love for the pulse of life!
When everything comes to cease
From His gaze of perfect love

To grasp at utter perfection:
To reach for the hand of Perfection Incarnate
And in return to be held by Love – ah, what Love!
My life is about to end, about to begin to the fullest!
When everything comes to cease
From His gaze of perfect love

To become a Saint is not as challenging as it may seem
When our trust remains always with Him
And when our souls sing the praise of the Eternal:
When everything comes to cease
From His gaze of perfect love
From indeed Love's own gaze, utterly perfect!

Part 9

The Book of Wisdom

Wisdom is the gift of understanding the world with a divinized perspective, catching a glimpse of God's mind and heart despite the comparatively narrow vision of man's capacity to know and love. Inspired by the Holy Spirit, a person with wisdom is able to see past the perceptions of reality and view reality itself – cause and end are accessible to the one with wisdom flowing from his heart. God Himself is the cause and end of man's existence, and so by a person understanding to a greater degree these truths about the nature of man, he or she perceives more profoundly the will of the Triune God.

The Book of Wisdom is found in sacred scripture, and so under normal conditions it would inherently fall under the category of Scripture, the first section of *My Soul Longs for You, My God*. Like the first section, it would be beneficial to read the Book of Wisdom before reading these poems, for scripture always precedes and is pre-eminent, and is far above these humble responses to the Word Himself. Examining the essence of these poems on wisdom, however, one can conclude that these nineteen poems need to be in a section of their own. After all, wisdom is that which every person seeks intellectually and beyond, even without being fully aware of it, for each person searches for the living God, the Giver of wisdom. It is the Lord, at all times, that holds all creation together by His Thought, by His Love.

There are nineteen chapters of the Book of Wisdom, and therefore there are nineteen poems in this ninth part of *My Soul Longs for You, My God.* These are not meant to be read only as a commentary to each chapter, however, for many of the themes of the Book of Wisdom consist of the Israelites' quest to remain righteous before God compared to their oppressors as the personification of man's tendency towards darkness. These poems should rather be read as exhortations written from a place within the soul of each person in the world, an interior place very close to the living God. Man indeed has the potential of realizing God dwelling within him, and thus he is able to experience the joy and suffering of Jesus Christ by drawing ever closer to Him. These poems are specifically a cry of encouragement to all of humanity to seek the wisdom of God at all times, no matter the circumstances, and to do so with right intentions. Life is too short to desire anything else above the Lord; with Him, all else is subordinate to His love.

The Lord extends to man His wisdom, and man either can reach forward and grasp at it with everything he has, or turn away and walk in the other direction. The former option provides man with the satisfaction and fulfillment he seeks at every moment, perhaps only to be realized later in life; the latter option gradually leads to self-destruction, for nothing can fully satisfy the heart of man but God Himself. Over the many millennia of his existence, man has developed new technology, founded nations, moved to every corner of the planet, and encountered new cultures and ideas along his journey. But yet the heart of man remains the same, seeking wisdom that only the Lord can provide. The journey to God is still man's final goal within the depths of his soul.

God the Father, embrace us as Your children.
God the Son, have mercy on us, sinners.
God the Holy Spirit, enflame our hearts with Your love.
And Blessed Mother Mary, carry us always to your Son.

Amen.

Wisdom 1

Seek God with sincerity of heart

From the depths of man
He acts, seeking eternity
In everything he does –
But by searching for God
Does he find Him?
Can he enter into communion
With the Divine?

It is not by actions first
That we find God,
But instead when we become
Content with only existing –
Nothing more,
Nothing less

When setting aside everything we do,
And simply rest with the Lord,
We find Him
Dwelling within us!
Right in front of us,
Behind us, above us,
Under us, *in* us
He has resided the entire time…

Oh, what grace flows forth
From Your love,
God my all,
What beauty and truth
Are perfected in You!

Upon realizing the secret of true fulfillment,
Embracing the concept from the heart,
Not only the mind,
That simply being is enough,
And that doing comes from being –
Not the reverse! –
We humbly ask our God to fill us,
And then receive His love

This is all we ever need in life:
The love of God our Father!
Why, then, do we preoccupy ourselves
With stress and anxiety?

If we let the Lord work in our lives,
Our actions for Him will surely follow
Our relationship with Him,
In Him

After being, comes thought –
Here we must be vigilant to maintain
The disposition of openness to the Lord,
For profane thoughts can stain the soul,
Disrupting the internal justice
The Lord has freely given

Perseverance is necessary
To think about Him and not dwell
On evil –
Actions rooted in His love
Follow naturally from pondering
His will day and night

Put aside every distraction, every
Foolish object,
Physically or spiritually!
Seek God with all your heart, never
Hesitating, but always
With eagerness and direction,
Both given by God Himself!

There is nothing to fear
When rooted in the Lord;
The yields of our souls, still standing
Despite the fierce winds,
Will be firm in the ground
Of righteousness,
And watered by the springs of wisdom,
To make them fertile
For the Lord's harvest

The Spirit of the Lord has filled the world

The Holy Spirit, the ever-generous
Giver of wisdom,
Perfectly merciful and just,
Provides all with Himself

At all times!
Seeing everything take place
According to the will of the Father,
Sent to enflame the hearts
Of all people

The Spirit is given to each
In accord with the Divine Mind
In of Itself;
Each receives the Spirit
In accord with his openness
And willingness to respond
To the gifts bestowed
With love and a generous heart

Then will the hearts of the Wise
Be enflamed, and the hearts
Of the foolish grow dormant –
Everything the Lord has given
Is to be used for His praise,
And not to be taken for granted
In both word and deed

He who has created each one of us
Can surely know every thought,
Hear every word,
And see every action we do –
In the eternal present!

This should not weigh us down,
But instead foster an internal
Sense of true freedom

We have the capacity
To live in accordance with how
We were made by God:
Ad maiorem Dei gloriam

Behold, everything we see, hear,
Smell, taste, and touch,
And also all we cannot perceive
Physically, but with the eyes of faith,
Has been created by the Living God!

By a unique thought of the Mind
Has every entity come into being
Except Himself who has always been
And will always be!

The responsibility lies with us, then,
Never to forget the wisdom
He has so graciously granted us,
And to use His strength
Not for personal gain like the ungodly,
But for the praise of God
Like the holy ones

The words we speak
Are meant to build,
Not to destroy

Let every word we utter be united
To the Word of God, Jesus Christ,
Who has sent Himself in the Holy Spirit
For the continuous renewal of His creation

Righteousness is immortal

Christ has given suffering and death
Meaning, depth, significance
For the rest of humanity,
Indeed for each one of us,
Both individually and collectively

Before, death entered the world
By the first sins of Adam and Eve,
Yet now man has been redeemed by Christ
To bring us to the fullness
Of life with God

But it was never in the active will
Of the Almighty God to have
Death permeate His creation;
We chose it for ourselves…

How beautiful it is,
How truly exalted is God
Upon the cross,
That in allowing this corruptibility
Through His permissive will,
The glory of the Almighty
Might be shown to humanity in love

And ultimately by taking the punishment
Of humanity's sin upon Himself,
The greatest good of all
Has come about,
Namely,
Christ Jesus rising from the dead!

Oh, the Mind that perceived
All of this at once,
And made such good come forth
From the most heinous of crimes!

Oh, the Heart that loved humanity,
Despite its fallen nature,
So much that even the most ungodly,
The most against Him,
Were still exonerated from the punishment
They earned

By the blood of Jesus Christ,
The Holy Spirit, the Love
Between the Father and the Son –
The Generator of wisdom
In the past, present, and future –
Can spark in every soul
A spiritual flame so powerful
That anyone can change his ways,
That anyone can live for the Good, the True,
The Beautiful Lord and God!

But will the fire within be maintained?
Will we put more logs
Into the depths of our hearts
Where the fire still persists?

To do so is to live
The righteousness that is itself
A gift from God

If we live for Jesus Christ,
The fire will not be extinguished
But instead burn ever brighter! –
And the just will enter
Into the glory of God
At the proper time,
Aligned ever precisely
By His eternal will

Live for God!
Seek the wisdom
Of His most Holy Spirit!
The choice now will surely
Resound in eternity,
For better or worse…
For God's praise,
Would that it be for the better,
Not only for ourselves
But also for the entire world!

Wisdom 2

Our name will be forgotten in time

The unjust of heart and mind
Live for themselves,
Investing in the world
Rather than in the Eternal God –
Shall they not render
The Lord what is due
To Him?

They regret the short duration
Of their lives;
Why would the opportunity
Of seeing God in the face
Sooner
Be not a cause for joy?

It is because they have forgotten
Who they have been made
To be

If the world forgets us
Like sand blowing in the wind
Because we have not lived for it,
But instead for God,
This is indeed a reason
To rejoice!

The world is temporary,
Passing away,
But God is eternal
And everlasting

We realize our mortality,
Our contingency, the most
When we do not live for ourselves

How beautifully paradoxical it truly is
That in the appearing weakness of mortality
God has brought us the chance for life with Him!

We cannot live with the Lord
Until we have died,
And we cannot be ready to die
Until we actively prepare
For that glorious moment

How have you chosen
To die for the Lord
Today?

For the unjust the increasing
Proximity of death frightens
And intimidates,
But to the just,
In love with wisdom,
No fear can touch the peace
Of God within them!

A spiritual death prepares a person
For the death of the body –
And ultimately death is but
The beginning of life eternal,
If we have lived for God now

Yes, *tempus fugit,*
Momento mori –
The stakes are too high
To disregard the next life,
For it comes knocking at the door
At the most unexpected hour:
So are the ways of the
Omniscient God

Let none of us fail
To share in our revelry

If we are not completely rooted
In the love of God,
Grateful for His generosity,
It means that we have not given back
To God enough, for He always gives to us

We have the capacity
By our own free will either
To seek the face of God
Or to not seek the divine

He does not coerce us,
But gently shows Himself to His creation
In the simple, in the peaceful,
In the melodious songs of silence

This is the true mark of omnipotence,
That God can bring goodness from
Even the most horrible evils
Of the world

We as human beings have been made
By God to seek Him
By our nature –
This makes it easier to do so
Because it is intrinsically a part
Of our humanity to look for God!

We indeed search for an answer
To the question of "why" –
And will look anywhere to find it

If not God, then where else?
Creation is not God Himself,
But instead *from* Him,
And *for* Him

Nevertheless, these things, though
Not transcendent by their very nature,
Can become like gods to us,
If we are not firm in the Lord

If we invest our time, energy, and talents
Into the things of the world,
We are effectively giving preference
To these *things*
Instead of the living, Triune God

How illogical!
How foolish!

But each and every one of us
Sins this way too often

We are fallen, in need of God's mercy,
But never without hope,
Never without the love
Of the Father

When we let these things
Govern the way we act,
We have crossed the line
From having these things be used
As tools according to their nature,
And instead make them
Ends in themselves

They require us to sacrifice for them:
To give of our time and effort –
Indeed, we worship these things…
In reality,
We are no better than the pagans

What is the difference between
A false god of the sun or moon,
And a "god" of money, technology,
Pleasure, our own glory,
And so on…?

My brothers and sisters
in the risen Lord
Jesus Christ,
We must be honest with ourselves,
And humble enough to recognize
That the pronoun "we" is undoubtedly
Appropriate here

We *all* have fallen into
These traps before in our lives…

We all have enjoyed the pleasures
Of the world, and this is good
Because God has made the world
And everything in it,
And made it all to be good!

But moderation is necessary –
Within the mental and emotional
Boundaries set by our spirituality:
Our souls for God merit the sacrifices
Against the pleasures of the world
So that we can live for Him!

Our bodies are temporary,
Able to decay;
Our souls are everlasting,
And will experience at some point
Either heaven or hell

Which will we choose?

Purgatory is a saving grace
From our merciful God,
But let us not live for the world now
And aim only for Purgatory!

Let us aim for Heaven
Immediately after death –
This is only possible
For a saint relying
Totally on God's help

This is indeed our calling;
This is indeed our cause for hope!

He professes to have
Knowledge of God

The conscience of man
Prevails, despite any iniquity committed –
It is written on the heart of every member
Of humanity: a fundamental
Recognition of right and wrong

This seed of the truth
In the heart informs the mind's conscience,
Directing it to search and find
The Truth,
Inasmuch as the heart is in tune
With the song of God's presence

When one lives for God,
In accord with his nature,
He is in harmony with himself,
And is open to the promptings
Of the Holy Spirit that the Father
Sends forth each day of his life

If one does not live for God,
He then looks for things that he perceives
Will fill him with the peace and joy
That only God can give –
In the end he still feels empty,
Unsatisfied, without happiness
In the ultimate sense of the word

He asks himself why there is still
A longing in his heart,
Why he yet has the desire for God
Within his soul

Living for God requires acting
In accord with His commandments:
When one, though imperfectly
Because he is human, lives this principle,
He shines with the very light
Of Christ Jesus,
And preaches Him as the Word
Not by words alone but
By his very life,
Confirmed by the Word!

Seeing this, the unjust man becomes anxious,
For the just man speaks to his soul
With the very Word of God

The message pierces the spot
Within him where his consciousness
Of God still remains,
Where the fire of conscience
Yet has a few embers left smoldering

The man living for God is perceived
As a threat by the unjust man,
For it is possible that he may need
To change his ways if he lets the light
Of that man shine into his soul

The light is not exclusively of the man *in se*
But the light of Christ radiating
Through him!

And so instead of listening well
To the man's whispers on behalf of
The living God,
The unjust man gathers his friends
To persecute the innocent one,
To ridicule the holy one

This is fulfilled in the Person
Of Jesus Christ Himself,
Who bore the immensity of our injustice
Willingly, without reserve or hesitation!

We can live by this same Light
By suffering for Him
In our own lives
Willingly, without reserve or hesitation,
Just as He did

Will we be the just or unjust person?
The choice is indeed given to us daily;
We know the consequences that will come
From either decision

Please, God, help me to choose the former!
Help me daily to testify to You,
Oh Lord, the eternal Truth –
Nothing else matters but You,
And the more You permeate my soul
With Your grace, the more I will be able
To glorify Your name with a selfless heart

They did not know
The secret purposes of God

Every time we step away from God,
Either from sin explicitly or complacency,
Which both hinder progress
To the Divine,
We misemploy our God-given
Intellect and will

Sin:
We say to ourselves that this thing,
Though not the Truth,
Is indeed truer than God is;
We say that we love this thing
Even more than we love *Him* –
Behold, the betrayal
Of our intellect and will

In the fulfillment of the Psalm,
We have all experienced time after time
What having eyes and ears but yet
Not seeing and hearing
Really means…

It is very easy to criticize others
When we begin on the journey to holiness,
But this is an error that slows our growth
In the Lord

All is His gift,
And what is required for us,
Upon receiving His generosity,
Is *humble gratitude*

This leads to the perfection
Of love within us

To give the Lord all we have
Is to give Him our entire lives:
He asks us to give Him
As simple a gift as that

Nothing more,
Nothing less

And it is said that God
Gives to no person what he
Cannot handle…
Yes, we are indeed being called
By the living God
To give all we have to Him
Because we are able to do so!

Trust in the Lord!
Because giving all we have to Him
Is not easy at all;
It is actually quite difficult,
Requiring many sacrifices here on earth
For the reward that awaits in heaven

But this reward is infinitely better
Than obtaining all the luxuries,
Pleasures, and honors
Of this world!

The reward Christ gives
To His just ones is eternal life

It requires wisdom to see this reality

Not with our eyes do we perceive
This great mystery,
But with our minds and hearts
United as one

Fides et ratio:
Faith and reason together,
Working as one!
To inform the other,
To complete the other,
Is Christ at the center –
The Truth sets us free!

Wisdom is the link between them,
Given as a gift from God,
To show us divine realities
To which both faith and reason
Can only but allude!

Indeed, the Apostle knew this intimately
When proclaiming to the Romans
With all his heart,
The "depths of the riches
And wisdom and knowledge of God"
That Jesus Christ revealed to him
Out of love,
And for his mission

We seek the face of the Lord;
We yearn for union and peace;
Let courage lead us to charity
On the road to the Divine!

Wisdom 3

Their hope is full of immortality

The just do not fear death;
They welcome the next step
On their journey,
That which will lead them to God

If one has lived a good life,
Rooted in God,
And has been open
To what the Lord has willed
To give him –
In the graces and sufferings both
(indeed many times
They are not
Mutually exclusive!) –
Then death is an exciting occurrence
For him:
To meet the One who has shaped his life
On earth, to whom it has been conformed

In order to gain the perfection of heaven,
We must first die;
In order to gain the perfection of heaven,
We must initially want to go there!
We must leave this world behind,
Not only physically
But spiritually first

Detachment from this world
In the modern age
Can certainly still mean
Living in the world

To live in the world
But not *of* the world
Is our evangelistic goal

This way, when the Lord calls us,
Each by name,
To Himself, we will neither mourn
Nor have fear,
But instead rejoice at the opportunity
To return home to our Father!

We are from and for
The Triune God

We indeed have such hope
For what is to come,
That which God only knows,
And that which we are called
To accept with love and patience,
With endurance,
With anticipation for His glory
To appear!

For who can probe the mind
Of the living God?
Who can know what is His plan?

Simply put, no one has the capacity
Unless God first showed him
For some purpose

And the Lord in His generosity
Does indeed show Himself to us –
He gives us life,
Both physically and spiritually!
This is not too removed from His
Very nature of self-giving Love

The world may look on the just
With misunderstanding,
Even contempt,
But God sees all things as they are

In their making, activity,
And end,
He is always present, maintaining
All in being by Himself!

Those who despise wisdom
And instruction are miserable

There is a difference between
Knowledge and wisdom,
Both philosophically and theologically,
That requires some wisdom
To understand in the first place,
Ironically enough:
A *sine qua non* to a certain degree

If one lacks wisdom,
He finds himself looking
For the answers of the universe
In the universe itself –
He searches for the satisfaction
Of knowing "why" in places where
Only "how" can be given to him

What he seeks, or more properly
Whom he seeks, of course, is God,
And without Him the individual
And all he knows – and also
What he does not know! –
Would cease to exist…

One who has wisdom is able to see
That his wisdom and knowledge
Are both not from himself,
But from God

With one only possessing knowledge,
The Evil One can convince him
That the knowledge he possesses
Comes from himself:
An utterly false lie
Originated indeed from
The Father of Lies!

Each person possesses some
Amount of knowledge *de facto*;
Fewer possess wisdom as well

Because many, though having the capacity
Given by God to embrace wisdom,
Have pushed it away

Each person has the capacity
To encounter within himself
The reasons for *how*
The things of the world are
The way they are;
Fewer have the openness
To realize *why* as well

But nevertheless the how and the why
Work together –
One without the other
Is a false absolute

But if one were to seek
To receive from the Lord one attribute
More than the other,
Let us echo Solomon who *prayed*
For wisdom,
And was granted that humble petition

Both knowledge and wisdom
Point to God –
Knowledge will lead to the desire
For more knowledge;
Wisdom will lead to the desire
For more of both!

Attaining wisdom means that one
Has encountered intimately
The Divine

The souls of the just
Are in the hand of God

With wisdom one has the ability
To see into the life of another,
Past the walls the person may have built,
And speak tenderly, with the voice of God,
Piercing the soul with fiery love!

The fruit of wisdom, therefore,
Is justice –
In both its practical
And absolute senses

When wisdom enflames the heart
By the power of the Holy Spirit
As a fire engulfs the wood
From which it gains its fuel
(so, too, does the Spirit choose
To work through us!),
We then have the Sight to perceive
The need for giving
To each what is owed him

"Give to Caesar what belongs to Caesar,
And give to God what belongs to God"

Give to man and God
What is due, respectively,
With the greater priority
Being directed, of course,
To the Creator of man

Those who are wise, by God's grace,
And therefore just,
Are able to walk with God
Each day with joy

Those who are wise, by God's grace,
And therefore just,
Have the potentiality to cease to live
For themselves,
And let the Lord overshadow them

Those who are wise, by God's grace,
And therefore just,
Give to the world a shining example
More than they ever
Could have accomplished
Alone
By abandoning themselves
To the holy providence
Of God!

The world often rejects
These holy men and women
Because they preach in the name
Of Jesus Christ a *message*

A message so counter-cultural,
So counter-intuitive,
That which would threaten
To disrupt the established paradigm
Of blissful ignorance,
Of complacency,
Of sin…

There is indeed no comfort
When the life we once lived
Is placed onto the cross
Of Jesus Christ,
With Jesus Christ!
No comfort can be experienced
There –
Only the suffering of the Servant

But it is there that the wise
Are most especially in the hand of God –
"No torment shall touch them"
Even though torment shall surely come,
Even though adversity will try to touch them
Unto death!

The peace gained by experiencing
The suffering and death of our Lord
Intimately within us:
An inner tranquility,
An interior embrace of love,
That which the comforts
Of the world cannot give!

From this death comes a newness of life –
For certainly those who are made
To live within themselves
The slaughter of the Lamb
Also, in turn, in God's time,
Experience His resurrection!

Oh Wisdom, Holy Spirit,
To You be the praise and honor
Of our lives forever

You have examined the heart
And, while yet still finding sin,
Have granted Your gifts
All the same –
Through Jesus Christ the Lord,
To the glory of God the Father

Amen.

Wisdom 4

The righteous, though they
Die early, will be at rest

Oh Lord, how much time
Have You given me to live
On this earth?

I yearn to use every moment
Of my life now, here, as an offering
To You, so that I might one day
Be united with You in heaven

But it would certainly help
To know how long this duration
Of life will be... I believe?
Or would I procrastinate instead?

Lord, I accept that only You know
How long You have allotted for me,
Indeed for all Your children

And I am content with knowing
Neither the day nor the hour,
Lest I take it for granted!

If it is Your will for me
To live until old age,
Let Your name be praised

If it is Your will for me
To die soon, younger than expected,
Let Your name be praised –
Your glory, oh Lord, is not contingent
On my existence at all

But if I could choose one over the other,
If You gave me the choice,
I would accept the latter with joy
Because I value life with You more
Than this current life I lead

To some this may sound concerning,
For the world encourages us
To live a life full of pleasure
And enjoyment
Because we only have one life to live…

But I say, in the name of Jesus Christ,
That since we do only have but
A single life before Judgment,
Live morally and upright before God!

It is not that I do not enjoy life here;
On the contrary, life is full of good
Because the Lord made it to be so –
But yet yearning with everything to see Him
In the face, the prospect of heaven
Will overshadow *anything*
The world would ever be able
To provide for me

The satisfaction of self-possession
In and through the Lord
Gives much greater happiness than
The world can supply,
Much greater peace
Than the turmoil felt inside

And so we must ask ourselves
Daily, with honest hearts,
About the life for which we
Are currently living:
Either for this life
Or the next

And yes, it indeed is one or the other,
Not both,
Because our Lord said Himself that
"we cannot serve both God
And mammon"

If right now, examining sincerely,
We are living only for this current life,
There is always the opportunity
To change!

There is always the chance
To live for God, to go to Him
With everything,
Not yet as we should be,
But as we are

The Lord wants us to be honest with Him
When we pray, even though
He knows us so much better
Than we know ourselves anyway

It is because being honest with Him
In prayer begins to create the interior disposition
To be more honest with ourselves in our daily lives,
A critical step on the road to holiness

And if the answer is the latter,
For the next life,
We go to the Lord in humility,
Asking Him to protect us so that
We remain on the path to Him
And not fall into behaviors contrary
To sanctification

We pray this from the heart
So that when He calls us
Home to Himself, ah!, that state
Of eternal rest,
We may enter into the realm of the Divine
With joy and peace –
With an inestimable happiness! –
Even if that day
Is tomorrow

Would we be ready tomorrow
If the Lord called us home?

The fascination of evil
Obscures what is good

The world is able to corrupt us,
Even though it has been made good
By God: it is clearly not the highest good,
Not even beginning to begin
To equal God!

Indeed, how can God create something
Equal to Himself? It is not possible;
All His creation is subordinate
To Him always

Thus, when we invest more of ourselves
Into the world instead of God,
We establish an internal disposition
That is closed off to God's promptings
In our lives,
Exactly how the Evil One wants it

Prima facie evil seems attractive,
Desirable, pleasurable,
Alluring

And it is indeed true, not *in se*,
But because the things that attract us
Are goods created by God,
Warped in perception by the Enemy

If we live according to our appetites
And emotions alone,
We will fall into these lesser goods
Over and over again –
Reason is needed always,
for it guides by prudence

Is this challenging?
But of course!
If this necessary?
Iterum verum est!

Thus we *know* by the God-given
Gift of our intellect that those
Things will neither satisfy our longing
For God nor help us
On our journey to Him!

We know it to be true,
And so this knowledge must remain
Stronger than the longings put upon us
By the world,
The flesh, and the Devil

Only this knowledge can guide us
To the Divine, in which wisdom
Is given to us on earth
To prepare us for heaven –
The eternal perfection of wisdom
When seeing her heart:
The heart of God!

But if even our knowledge
Has been corrupted by the Devil
Using the world's allurements,
What is necessary is to start over again

To return to the Lord as a child!

Would that this be a daily occurrence
For us, to go to the Lord as children,
Seeking His mercy, forgiveness,
And love!

The Lord will indeed forgive!
He will indeed begin to transform
And purify even the most warped
Parts of our souls if we let Him
Do so, if we let ourselves
Be vulnerable

God's grace and mercy are
With His elect

The chosen of God are not perfect
By any figment of the imagination

The saints throughout history
Have been quite sinful at times,
Full of expanses within them
Needing love and healing

But they continued to return to the Lord
As His beloved sons and daughters,
Yearning to be embraced by their Father
And ours! –
They did not leave the battlefield
In the war for their souls
With the Enemy fighting them day after day

And with this way of life,
God spares these men and women
From much corruption
Because He sees in them the *desire*
For holiness, for Light –
This longing is already an immensely
Significant step toward God
To which we are all called!

We, too, can be saints
With the help of God

We, too, can bring Jesus Christ
To the world as the saints have done
Throughout the centuries

Truly, God calls everyone to the glory
That is holiness! No one can be too sinful
So as to be denied this blessing from
Our all-generous God!
What is required of us, however,
Is the yearning for holiness
In the first place

If we have been given this desire now,
Let God be praised!
Pray that this not only remains
Rooted in our hearts
But grows ever stronger

If there is not yet that desire
Within us,
Do not be afraid!
Today can be the day to return
To the Lord of all
With all we have

But be well advised:
Just as the holy men and women
Of God who are taken into His glory
Did not know the day or the hour,
So we too do not know when that day
Will come –
And it surely will come!

Should we wait for the
"Proper" moment to return to God
And risk missing it completely
When the Lord calls us,
Each by name, out of this world
Into the next?

No, seek the Lord *today and always*!

Wisdom 5

What has our arrogance profited us?

Every human being is equal to another
By the very congruency of nature
That they share:
One has been brought into the world
Not by his own power,
But by the providence of God,
And will leave the world
In the same way

So, too, for the other,
And for every person in the world

Those who are arrogant
Have no right to be;
Only the Lord has the right
To say that He is all-powerful,
All-knowing, far above all things
(Which is all indeed true!) –
But He still does not speak with arrogance!
God is humble, simple,
Loving

Arrogance means trusting oneself
Over others, perhaps even over God;
It is an over-confidence
In one's abilities

This can apply not only to
Our daily lives and occupations,
But also to the spiritual life:
We must be careful,
Ever vigilant against the Evil One

An effect from arrogance over time
Is the gradual diminishment of charity:
Without charity one is
An empty shell…
He who walks with arrogance,
With a prideful heart,
Will never be satisfied
With what he has,
And will deny that he lacks
What he does not have

The arrogant one lives interiorly
For himself and to himself,
And sows the same seeds of deception
To God in prayer,
If he still prays at all…

But God sees all things
As they actually are, not
By how they appear –
The Lord is all-knowing,
Full of power, and yet we still think
We can hide from Him,
Think we can overpower His will
By our own stubbornness

And the intriguing notion
Is that God, because of His
Omnipotence and omniscience,
Many times allows us to be that way,
As we act like unbroken mules,
So that we ourselves might experience
The consequences of our own actions

Do not be fooled into believing
That all we are is a hopeless,
Egotistical aggregate of matter

How beautiful it is that despite our failures
The Lord remains faithful to us,
Loving us still:
Never ceasing to give,
Never ceasing to embrace us
As His sons and daughters!
Let Him be praised forever

We had no sign of virtue to show

Yes, we are the beloved children
Of God who delights in us!
Although arrogance can drive us
Away from Him over time
By our own choice to act thus,
There still is never a place
Where the Lord is not present,
Calling us back Home

Although we can sin so as
To diminish or even take away
Our capacity to receive the grace of God
For a period of time,
Nothing we ever do can increase or decrease
The love God has for us! –
It is constant and equal
For every person whom He
Maintains in existence

But nevertheless this identity as beloved
Sons and daughters of the Most High
Does not fully exonerate us from the evil
We have done against Him –
That is why there is salvation in Christ
And sanctification in His Church;
The beautiful Sacrament of Confession
Gives us great hope indeed!

Without this Sacrament, however,
From where can hope come
Outside of Christ working in the Sacrament
Itself?

The Lord desires for us
To go to Him with sorrow and repentance
From the sins we have committed, of course,
But the sins remain
Until we go to Confession
And encounter Christ Himself
Through the priest *in persona Christi*

If the holy men and women of God
Still struggle with sin in their lives,
While receiving the Sacraments regularly
And doing penances,
How is it possible for someone
Who does not receive our Lord
To succeed in his fight against evil?

It would be like a horse
Running a race without a jockey
To guide it –
There is no consistent direction, no lasting purpose
Without Jesus Christ
To lead us

Indeed, what a pity it is that when
We enter that pattern of living
(every Saint, being a sinner,
Has experienced this as well)
We truly have no virtue to show!
In order for virtue to develop,
Practice and repetition of good actions
Is necessary

It is right and just to reflect often
On the Sacraments,
Those outward signs instituted by Christ
To His Church, the most efficacious way
For us to receive His grace

Do not be mistaken that those
Who have not received the Sacraments
Regularly, or even at all,
Are doomed to eternal punishment

No, of course not,
But living without the help of the Church
Makes the journey that much
More arduous

Acknowledging the Lord spiritually
Is another way to Him, but a longer route it is…
Even the staunchest atheist
Can still be living for God
Even if he does recognize God
As who He is

But it is harder yet,
A longer road to be travelled,
A steeper precipice to avoid
If failure comes on the way

Without God, we truly have no virtue
To show to anyone at all,
But *with Him* all things
Can be accomplished
According to His plan

To Him be glory forever and ever!

But the righteous live forever,
And their reward is with the Lord;
The Most High takes care of them

It is precisely when we die to ourselves
In this world that we begin to live
More fully,
In Jesus Christ our Lord

It is precisely when we actually die
That we will enter the fullness of life
With God, provided that we have died
To ourselves by then, provided that
We have become holy
By the grace of God

What glory awaits us if we but desire it;
The Lord will not ever deny
A soul the gates of Heaven if the soul
Genuinely seeks it

There might be
Some time spent in Purgatory for purification,
But the soul will be preserved from the eternal fires
Of Hell, those unquenchable, terrible fires…
From the bottom of my heart
I cry out to all of humanity
That we need to remember that
We will indeed be judged one day:
Death comes to us all

It is perhaps the reality in *this* world
About which we can be the surest;
The reality about which we can be surest
Overall is God's love for us

The Lord, the Just Judge, will certainly provide
For each soul a verdict of both complete
Justice and mercy, flowing forth
From His heart of love and mercy
That we ourselves have pierced
By our sins

The righteous will in time gain
What they have earned by living
A just, holy life –
Not by themselves, however,
Have they accomplished this feat,
But by relying on the grace of the Lord:
By being an open vessel
To the outpouring love of the Father

We all will die someday…
Yes, our time here is only temporary,
With limit, finite!

But the next life is everlasting,
Be it either heaven or hell;
My prayer is that no soul ever
Chooses to go to hell again!
Instead, that each person listens to the gentle
Voice of the Lord calling out with love

"I love you"

"Return to me"

"You are my beloved"

"I love you!"

Let many conversions, oh Lord,
Occur today! Let Your mercy
Be experienced in every heart,
Almighty and Everlasting
And Ever-loving God!

You take care of all of us,
Oh Lord, holding us all in existence

Would that every person
In the world hear the Name
Of Jesus Christ! Would that
Every person thus hear
The Truth!

Behold, the darkness is fleeing;
The light growing ever brighter
And stronger is permeating
Every soul!
Radiance of the Father's love,
This light heals every affliction
Of the heart,
Every infirmity of the spirit:

Oh, the mercy and love of God!

We fall down in adoration
Before the Lamb who was slain,
Beholding His simplicity *and* glory
Simultaneously

May He be praised at all times,
By all peoples,
For all time!

Amen.

Wisdom 6

So that you may learn wisdom
And not transgress

Wisdom speaks the truth
To the heart, sent by God
To enflame one's life with love and hope,
If we but accept the wisdom
Into ourselves from Him

Growth in the understanding
Of the Divine naturally
Creates within us the capacity
For more holiness, if we but
Accept the growth
Into ourselves from Him

The Lord has won the war
Against Satan upon the cross,
Giving us salvation through
His own blood, but we then
Must live according to this sacrifice
If we are to enter into life with Him

We are not bound by darkness
If we but accept the light
Into ourselves from Him

This light shines brightly,
Carrying power in itself for
Repentance and conversion –
We know this power is not
From us but Him, and we can receive it
If we but accept the power of Christ
Into ourselves from Him

These gifts that Jesus desires to give us
Will slowly transform our lives,
Crushing our sins in His own blood,
So that we might never again
Transgress against the Lord

We are human, imperfect:
Yes, we will fall again and again
Still, but over the course of our lives
Fewer and fewer times,
And with less severity –
The gradual conformation of our hearts
To His!

This path to wisdom, and thus to God,
Is a cyclical journey:
Accepting the gift of wisdom
When God provides it will lead
To growth in the spiritual life;
This brings greater light to one's existence,
Which provides power to accept
Yet more wisdom in our lives

This cycle, as with all circular processes,
Has no definite beginning or end –
And we are open to the gifts
That the Lord desires to give,
We journey closer to eternity with Him

There are many entry points in this cycle,
For there is no set beginning location;
The Lord can work how He desires!
Perhaps He gives a power of some type:
This will lead to wisdom
And the rest of the journey

This can be applied to the Gifts
Of the Holy Spirit, the Charismatic
Gifts of the Holy Spirit, and also to
Receiving wisdom from Him in general:
In all three of these cases,
We are the ones who *receive*
From the Lord what He chooses
To give to us

Receive in order to give

For what can man give to God
So as to add to Him?
Even giving Him praise
And thanksgiving does not add
To His inherent glory!

We are called to praise and thank Him
Nevertheless because He loved us first,
And responding in love, give back to Him
After receiving His life!

Giving heed to her laws
Is assurance of immortality

Obedience can be discussed intellectually;
It can be analyzed and understood
By the mind rather easily
In its conceptualization

But how frequently do we
Live obedience from the *heart*?

Obedience requires docility and humility,
Two characteristics that signify
A person to be already close to God –
Counter-cultural indeed these
Qualities are today!

Obedience to one's superiors
Is necessary not only for order
In the workplace but also the
Interior openness to the Lord:
If one struggles with the former,
He will certainly struggle with the latter,
For God does ask much of us at times
But never more than we can handle!

Obedience to the Lord, in fact,
Demands gently (ah, the paradox!)
A complete death to self, a total
Abandonment to the will of God –
And surprisingly this is
More practical than any agenda
Of ours

If I still have my own ideas
About how to live my life
That are contrary to God
And His will for me,
I might still act on these ideas
Because the Lord will never
Force me to obey Him

But by doing so I make myself
Empty, a shell
Instead of the full person
The Lord wants me to become!

And here lies the beautiful reality
That is at the heart of obedience
In all forms, but especially to the Lord:
Obedience is lived out of love
For Him!
Not by being forced or coerced,
But by being led by the hand of God
To a further, deeper love for Him,
We are able to say yes to the Lord
Freely, without hesitation

This is true freedom!
This brings a soul to true happiness!

And wisdom is needed in one's soul
To discern these truths accurately

The Lord will give this marvelous
Gift to those who ask Him:
"Knock, and the door
Shall be opened"

Obedience is the love of the wounded,
Dying Jesus, who remained faithful
To His Father's will through death!
Jesus, help me to be obedient to You
As You were to Your Father,
Even if this fidelity
Means suffering of my own
For You

Already I feel You guiding me,
Oh Lord, to your Mother,
The seat of wisdom, full of grace!

What intimacy You gave to her, and now
Give to us through her in the spirit
Of Your holy wisdom!

Mary, *sedes sapientiae*,
Pray for us always.

Honor wisdom, so that
You may reign forever

We can never know fully
The mind of God, even in heaven –
We only will ever see glimpses
Of His nature, glances into
The core of Being itself

And in heaven this will supply
For us happiness that will satisfy every
Desire in our hearts:
In heaven, we will no longer want to know God
Fully because of fear and trembling in His presence!
We will be more than content
With what He reveals
To us for all eternity!

And so how can we arrive
At this glorious Destination?
How can we travel this
Arduous journey
And also maintain inner peace?

By the grace of the Father
Given by the Son through the
Holy Spirit,
All things are possible

What has happened is already past;
What will occur will soon come to be

And so we are left in the present,
Deciding here and now
How to live our lives for God

Honoring wisdom is done
Without hesitation,
And giving thanks to God
Is done without reserve;
The end of our life
Comes without warning;
The judgment to be experienced
Does not come without cost

But we can go to Jesus through Mary:
When we honor wisdom,
We honor her because she
Bore the living God
In her womb –
Of course she deserves our respect
And honor,
As any mother merits,
But to the fullest extent of our effort!

Mother of God yet perpetual virgin,
Born without Original Sin
And eventually assumed body and soul
Into heaven –
We love you, Mother Mary,
And adore your Son
Through you!

The simplicity of life comes
With knowing our identity –
Our essence as human beings originates
From the Father, and will return
To Him:
Simplicity given by God
Who is perfectly simple!

To honor wisdom means to rest
With this simplicity before God
Each and every day,
So that we may gain
By His grace the gates of heaven
To dwell forever with the
Eternal Divine Love!

Wisdom 7

I called on God, and
The spirit of wisdom came to me

Oh, Shepherd of my heart,
You know my thoroughly,
For being formed by Your hands
Gives me inherent dignity
As a beloved son of You,
The Ever-loving Father

Oh, that I might approach You
Willingly, with joy and peace,
To testify to the world
The wonders You have done for me,
The marvels You have indeed shown
To every person in the world,
The simplest and yet most profound
Being the gift of life itself

Calling out to You implies
My vulnerability

Weakness, frailty: humanly unpopular
To be weak and in need, but spiritually
Necessary every day!

When this vulnerability,
This abandonment, this surrender,
This light of wisdom permeates
Any soul, the peace of God
Prevails over the darkness
Of sin and death!

And when Your spirit, sweet wisdom,
Indeed comes to me,
I watch as a humble bystander
As You draw me out of myself
Into Your radiant light

And from this beautiful attainment
Of simple glory You give so generously,
I slowly learn to accept my place
Not only as an instrument (barely
Even as this, oh Lord, You know me well!)
But also, and primarily,
As one of Your sons
Forever more

I love her more than
Health and beauty

Wisdom is of God,
Who is outside of time:
Eternal, everlasting, unchanging
Indeed is the Almighty
Triune God

But the things of this world
Are temporary: neither eternal
Nor everlasting, and certainly
Able to change over time,
Certainly able to pass away

The one who loves wisdom
Somehow enters into a place
Within himself that transcends
These worldly things, and
Is closely in tune with
The voice of God

In tune with the silence
Of most profound eloquence!

Your wisdom, oh Lord,
Is so sweet, so enriching,
That I now find time away from her
To be empty and insignificant

I desire deeply to learn
More about her, and how
She can bring me to You

It is not only from my mind
That I can see that loving wisdom
Is more profitable, more fitting,
Than loving the things of the world,
And therefore discern to act accordingly

No, I also love wisdom from the heart
(in fact, from the heart is the only
Way to love truly!),
Longing to give myself
To her insights that come
Directly from the heart of God

Oh, the yearnings of my soul
To enter into the fullness
Of wisdom,
To see her as she is,
A product of the very Mind of God!

Not limited by corporeal restrictions,
She moves freely because of her identity
As the perfect vessel of the Holy Spirit,
And thus He shares her (indeed, He shares Himself!)
With those whom He wishes,
In accord with His divine plan

Oh wisdom, embrace me today
By the power of the Holy Spirit!
For I am lonely without you;
Embracing you gives me understanding
To know that I am gradually
Approaching the Almighty God
In my life,
That I am progressing
On the journey of holiness

For she is a breath
Of the power of God

Wisdom carries with her no burdens;
Subtle and agile are her movements,
For she comes from the Most High,
Not hindered by any corporeal limitations
That we human beings have

The Holy Spirit, the love
Between the Father and the Son,
Ad intra, sends forth
The beautiful aspiration of wisdom
To all His creation

Our souls thus breathe in the light fragrance
Of the knowledge of God!

No one can fully understand God,
And so knowledge of Him
Comes from Himself through the gift
Of wisdom only in small portions,
And only on occasion

But these instances of realizing
From within ourselves the greatness of God
Provide more joy and excitement
Than anything the world
Could potentially bring to us!
God is always good!

We breathe to live each day;
If the Lord would take away our breath
From us, we would die,
As the Psalms beautifully
Remind us

Pause for a moment with the beauty
Of how wisdom is the very breath of God,
The Holy Spirit, giving life to all it encounters,
Ad extra from the unity of the Most Holy Trinity!
We need not see this reality
With our eyes, but instead understand it
With our hearts by faith

This surpasses the physical perceptions
Of the world, making them only tools
To find God present in His creation

Wisdom gives her insight
To the soul with gentle whispers,
Guiding the soul to God
With every word she utters:
And this word is always the same!

What is this word she speaks?
It is indeed nothing other
Than the very Word of God,
Jesus Christ,
Our Lord and Savior!

Wisdom 8

I desired to take her
For my bride

The moment I lost myself,
By my own choice through
The emptying of my will to God,
I found her

And how beautiful wisdom really is;
How graceful are her ways;
How honest and true
Is every word she speaks!

I have come to realize
How little I really know
Without her

Facts, figures, and the like
Lead me to God, surely, but
In of themselves they do not satisfy

Wisdom, however, shines her light
Upon my mind and heart,
Her brightness not of herself
But instead of her Lord and God,
Our King

See how wisdom surrounds the saints
With her guidance and protection,
Showing them the way
Through the darkness to reach
The most beautiful of all,
Our loving God

The saints are overshadowed by
Her graceful elegance

And realizing how much
She has done for me
By the power of God
In directing me to Him,
I desired to pursue her for marriage,
A deeper intimacy to be gained
With her, and thus God

What can I do to present myself
Well before her?

What is necessary for me to do
To earn her hand?

Surely wisdom herself
Would know the difference
Between flattery and true affection,
Between selfish desire
And genuine love…

In friendship with her,
Pure delight

Wisdom is pure, her ways
Being without blemish –
To be around her lifts my heart
To the Lord our God!

I feel deep within me
The presence of the Holy Spirit
When I spend time with her –
Of course, this is natural,
For it is He
Who gives her as He wills

My heart thoroughly rejoices
And my soul is indeed glad

My eyes yearn to see
Her enlightening smile once more,
And sing the praise of God
When they but glimpse her joyful face!
How can I not rejoice
When she exudes joy perpetually?

So close to God she is
That joy is the only product –
And this enters into my heart
Every instance I find myself
With her

For in her is found peace
At the understanding that comes
From her lips –
Nothing less than transcendence
Is issued from her mind; nothing less
Than love, the insight of the
Living God, shines forth from her heart

The relationship I have with wisdom
Has slowly been purified by the Lord:
Although initially I had the good desire
To marry her, it was tainted
With the lust pressuring me
To take only for myself

Now in friendship, oh Lord,
With Your wisdom I encounter
Your majesty,
For no longer do I want
To take her;
I only seek to share her
With all whom I meet,
For she comes from the living God,
And she seeks to guide every soul to Him!

But somehow I know in my heart
(Perhaps by wisdom's guidance!)
That there may be more purification
In the future
Needed within me still

But I perceived that
I would not possess wisdom
Unless God gave her to me

Where are you, my dear?
Where have you gone,
Oh my sweet?
Wisdom, have I offended you?
Please return, I pray,
To my soul

And upon this request I feel
Within me, from a place
I know not where, but still know
Surely exists, a warmth growing
In my soul that I have never
Experienced before

Could it be her loving embrace
Once more?

Then in the eloquence of God's silence
She spoke to me

Her word she gave to my soul
Was solace, grace, but not of herself inherently;
Her embrace of love was also not
Her own but both from another

From Another!

Indeed, both the Word
And the Embrace
Were Jesus Christ!

This was the final purification
In my befriending of wisdom,
The last step to take to God with her

I know profoundly now
That God Himself gives wisdom
To those who simply ask Him

Passively seeking her as opposed to actively –
In a spiritual sense –
Those who acknowledge their vulnerability,
Realizing that they lack her,
Go to the Lord in humility,
Asking Him to bestow her
Upon them

And the Lord indeed grants her thus!
Wisdom, you who see the very depths
Of the living God,
Emanating from His heart,
Guide me to Him always

And so in this process of gaining, losing,
And gaining her again in purity,
Her hand was at work the entire time

How beautiful it is that God guides *her* hand
At every moment,
Showing *her* the way
To enflame the heart of man

The Lord surely knows how
To work among His creation!

Wisdom 9

I am Your servant

Domine, non sum dignus
Ut intres sub tectum meum,
Sed tantum dic verbo,
Et sanabitur anima mea

These words encompass, oh God,
My nothingness before You,
But my confidence in Your love and mercy
Moves my heart to joy

Lifted up beyond the void
I can now see more clearly
Your purpose for me

Lord, let me always remain
Faithful to the special calling
You have given me:
To be Your servant

The world is already losing
Its desire to serve,
And so, too, will its
Capacity to serve eventually
Cease to be?

May Your will be done, oh Lord;
As Your servant I do not merit
Or even seek to know what lies ahead,
But You have nevertheless shown me
Because of this docility
Which is itself Your gift to me!

For when I think about how much
You have given to me, Your very unworthy servant,
I realize how much merit I lack
Because of my sins!

And this drives me to action
In Your name to combat
This darkness, not only
In my own life, but in the entire world!

Even in the darkest of times,
Your light never leaves;
Even when it seems that despair
Is the only response to such
Hatred, violence, and destruction
In the world,
You still bring hope to all!

Lord, You bring Your humble servant,
Weak and sinful,
Into Your presence –
And for this I am quite literally
Eternally grateful!

Who can learn the counsel of God?

Knowledge beyond knowing,
And wisdom beyond comprehension;
Joy beyond rejoicing,
And peace beyond contentment –
The Lord God works
In these ways, yet we know not
How or why

In the stillness of silence
We encounter the understanding
To be open to the ways
Of the Lord
(Only by peering into a mirror,
Not nearly in a direct way!)
And the love to embrace
The tranquility He gives our souls

But as for His counsel
And motives for doing all
He chooses to do,
We cannot even begin
To fathom the conception
Of any of it!

He is God,
And we so clearly are not:
In fact, we are very far away
From Him at times

But He loves us anyway,
Giving us Himself unconditionally

Behold, what a patient, generous, and truly
Loving God we are able to call
Father!

In all that we do,
Let us give glory to God
For how He has made us
His beloved children

In reciprocal Love, then
(Not in quality or quantity,
But proportionally, as much as we
Feeble human beings can give Him!),
We approach the Triune God
With songs of praise and thanksgiving
Ringing from our very souls

Wisdom 10

They passed wisdom by

To think that many people
Prefer the ways of the world
Over the ways of God…

Are we among these people
At times as well?

If we honestly answer, we already
Know the truth:
We are human, fallen from sin,
And thus far from perfect

Therefore, yes, in our lives
We have chosen the former over the latter
Again and again

This realization is not meant to condemn us,
But simply show each one of us
The dichotomy that lies
In front of us daily:
To choose God,
Or not to choose God

Are we able to find God
Working in His creation?
But of course!

He created all things inherently good,
Originating from Himself who is
Goodness itself,
And also constantly moves in our lives

But if we choose His creation
Over Him, we are making
A tragic error that leads us
Down the road to not choosing
Him at all

Indeed, tragic it is: the Lord
Never wants anyone to choose
Condemnation upon himself!
God truly loves us all so much
That He will allow people
To use their free will to live
For everything else instead of Him –
This is the essence
Of self-sacrificial love!

People pass wisdom by
Either by complete *ignorance*
Of her very existence,
By *apathy* in choosing lesser goods
Over her intentionally,
Or also by *weakness* in feeling torn
Between her and worldly things,
But not having the magnanimity
To sacrifice those things
On her behalf

Oh, the sad song of mourning
Their souls groan without their minds
Ever realizing it!
For when they deny wisdom's invitation,
Often implicitly,
They are only a few steps on the journey
From denying the Lord Himself,
The Giver of wisdom

She gave to holy people
The reward of their labors

The saints, too, have passed wisdom by
During their lives; they were human beings
As well, remember: imperfect, sinful,
And at times chose the ways of the world
Consistently over the ways
Of the Lord

But when wisdom came to them,
Extending her sweet invitation
To help them find the Lord,
Slowly each in his or her turn
Accepted this offer from wisdom,
And returned to the living God!

The saints never ceased fighting
For virtue, for holiness,
Indeed for God Himself!

They may have lost battles
In the war for their souls
Against the Evil One,
But they possessed the humility
To let the Lord fight for them,
And thus the war was won for them
By *His* hand!

We are also called to this victory;
We are being drawn by God
To this magnificent glory!

Never let the Devil tell you
That you are not holy enough
Or strong enough to become a saint,
Or that you have done too many bad things
To offend God that it is already too late –
These are lies from the Evil One!
If you are open to the Lord's grace,
You can indeed become a saint as well!

If we genuinely seek this crown
Of sainthood for pure reasons –
That is, to become holy
Through God and for God –
Then the Lord will indeed send His wisdom
To us in His time, providing us
The reward of our labors in His vineyard

But will we yearn for this
Universal calling wholeheartedly?

Nothing less than full commitment to God
Is required to obtain this crown;
Nothing less than complete dedication,
Reliance, and abandonment to the King
Is necessary for us to live!

Does this seem daunting?
It should!
That is why it is so beautiful:
To those who climb the mountain
To holiness, the Lord supplies graces
Beyond measure

So many did not even see
This path in their lives;
Many others saw it but did not take it;
Only a few chose to walk
The steep, narrow way to God,
And out of those fewer still
Continued the entire journey!

But those who remained faithful
Received their reward in Heaven!
We are called to this same trial
And also this same reward!

Wisdom 11

When they were thirsty,
They called upon You

In every period of history
And in every culture,
People have always asked for You
To support, help, and guide them
When in adversity –
And despite all appearances,
They continue to do so today

When the Israelites were in need of water,
They called upon Your generosity and love,
And You always heard the cry
Of Your people!
Every person in the world
Is a son or daughter to You:
The universe is indeed held
In the palm of Your hand

Today, though humanity has made
Progress technologically and socially,
We are still the same
As everyone else in history:
The fact remains that
We did not bring ourselves
Into being, and we will not leave
This world by our own power either

Behold, the solidarity of humanity
Found in shared weakness
And contingency!

And so because of this
Undeniable fact, we all are in need
Of a loving God and Father;
Approaching Him for help
Should not be such a painful endeavor
As many make it today

He will never reject us!
He will never deny us!

It takes a two-fold humility
To go to God with our needs –
First, to admit that we are thirsting
In some way, and second,
To ask God to guide us
Instead of trying to do everything
Ourselves

When we try to do everything ourselves,
We fail!

We are not strong enough,
But God is!

You are merciful to all,
For You can do all things

God is not some vindictive,
Hateful, destructive Being
Who loves to see us fail;
This would be inherently against His nature,
Against His essence of pure love!

We know this not only by the public revelation
Of Scripture, not only by the tradition
Of the Church founded by God Himself
In the Person of Jesus Christ,
But also in God's beautiful creation!

Behold, the intrinsic beauty
Of the sun setting over a tranquil lake,
The trees around it casting the shadows
Of dusk with so eloquent a silence

This directs us to God's beauty,
But does not encapsulate it:
God is infinitely more beautiful
Than that

Behold, the intrinsic beauty
Of a person's smile giving light
To another out of charity,
The offering of Jesus Christ
In the simplicity of a human gesture
So often overlooked!

This directs us to God's beauty,
But does not encapsulate it:
God is infinitely more beautiful
Than that

Behold the intrinsic beauty
Of Jesus Christ upon the cross,
Exemplifying the self-sacrificial love
That we are all called to have for Him!

This indeed directs us to God's beauty,
For it is the most beautiful experience
For us to witness here on earth –
God Himself dying for us out of love –
But *still* God is infinitely more beautiful
Than even that

We see Your mercy, Lord, upon the cross,
And also Your justice;
You can do all things,
And so therefore help us
Daily
To trust in You all the more

Wisdom 12

Your strength is the source
Of righteousness

Oh Lord, You are indeed worthy
To receive glory, honor, and power!
No one can escape Your piercing gaze,
Just as no one can elude death
Which comes upon all people
According to Your time

You give hope when there appears
No reason to maintain optimism

You bring light when there appears
No reason to battle against
The approaching darkness

You grace us with life
When we have not earned it,
Where there appears no reason
For You to act generously

And You provide all things by Your strength,
Inherently present with You,
At all times without fail –
Behold, this is most perfectly exemplified
On the cross!

Oh, great mystery of sacrifice!
Oh, suffering redemptive,
Tranquility arduous!
Teach me, Lord, to accept
My own cross as You did for me

If Your strength is that which
Gives You righteousness, and Your strength
Is always actualized, then You are always
Righteous and just – but also merciful!

We owe You our eternal gratitude

Everywhere I go You are there;
Every time I think You know it intimately,
Far better than I;
Every hair on my head has been numbered

Oh Lord, omniscient God,
Help me to accept my lack of strength
And therefore lack of righteousness!

I need *Your* strength
To carry on, oh Lord,
For without You I can do nothing

With *Your* strength
I will possess righteousness
And thus journey to You;
You will have to carry me
The entire way

They saw and recognized
As the true God the One whom
They had before refused to know

It is inevitable that every person
Will come to realize the existence
Of God at some point –
Either in this life on earth
Or in the next

If the moment of realization
Comes in the former, let the name
Of Jesus Christ be praised – the road
To Him in Heaven would have just begun,
Not ended!

And if this moment comes in the latter,
We pray for the mercy of God
To be supplied – and He is indeed
Perfectly merciful, but also perfectly just
Simultaneously

How can You be infinitely
Merciful and just at the same time,
Oh Lord my God?

Only You know, for it is a mystery
To all Your children:
We think justice and mercy
Are mutually exclusive

This is how we live,
But Your ways are not our ways…

Jesus, I cry tears of love
For You from within my soul,
In recompense for my own sins
And for every person's failures
Throughout the course of history –
Oh, that all might approach
Your Sacred Heart and experience
Your endless love for them!

Let this be always,
Without end,
When all things come to cease
At the glorious Sight
Of Your love for all

Wisdom 13

*The Author of beauty
Created them*

Oh sing to the Lord,
All you peoples!
Glorify Him with all you have,
For justice demands that you give Him
All in return for all He has given you

But it should not be only
A matter of justice:
The Lord is kind and merciful,
And full of generosity –
Ultimately, we are called to give all
We have to Him *out of love*,
Freely, with joy and peace
In our hearts

If we behold the inherent beauty
Of a single human being
It is more than enough to show
Your design, oh Lord,
The Author of beauty

For each has been made
In Your image, each
In Your wondrous likeness

Although we can never begin
To compare with You, the truth
We accept – and embrace! –
Is that You are our Father, Lord God

For indeed to whom have You given
Full merit of Yourself?
To no one but Your only begotten Son,
Jesus, whom You sent, Father,
For our salvation!

Shout for joy, therefore,
All nations of the earth!

Think outside your borders,
And live beyond the present age!

For the Lord will come one day,
And all the established economic,
Social, and political paradigms
Will count for nothing
If charity is extinguished from man's heart

Be vigilant!
Keep watch!
Do not let yourself invest too much
Of your time into the things of the world,
For when Beauty emerges in glory,
All that seemed beautiful here on earth
Will appear dreadfully bland
In comparison

Have courage, oh peoples!
The solidarity of humanity
Shows the glory of God among us –
The cross of Christ saved us all,
And there is nothing that can prevent
The Lord's plan of mercy and forgiveness
In the past, present, *and* future

Receive the Lord Jesus
In the Eucharist: welcome Beauty
Into your very body, and have Him rest
In your soul!
There is nothing more simple,
And yet profound;
There is no one more vulnerable,
And yet powerful!

As wisdom permeates the stubborn
Hearts of man, she embraces
The weaknesses and pain, bringing all
Suffering to the foot of the Cross

Returning smile for smile,
And embrace for embrace,
Man gradually becomes more comfortable
With wisdom's company, who is so very close
To the Living God,
Indeed to the Author of beauty
Who perpetually shares Himself with us

Wisdom 14

Blessed is the word by which
Righteousness comes

The holy name of Jesus
Penetrates all, wiping away
Any discord and lack of peace
By simply uttering His name
With respect and loving awe

It is no wonder why so many
Abuse His name, taking it in vain,
Because it has intrinsic power
And authority

This name, the Word Himself,
Has remained with His Church,
His bride, for two millennia,
And will continue to do so

Although we are sinful people
Who constitute the Church's members,
Christ is the Word by which
Righteousness comes to His beloved bride

And there lies inherent beauty
Directly from the mind of God!

He allows us to be the members
Of His Church – indeed, His very body! –
Even though we are far from perfect,
Far from Him

Who are we to approach
The Lord in the Eucharist?
We would not dare unless
He had first told us to come to Him

And He did!

With the darkness of this world
Growing every day, and with more people
Turning away from their loving God
Who does truly see their every action
And know their every thought,
We must be vigilant in preaching
Our Lord Jesus Christ!

Fully divine He is, of course,
But also fully human

The Word has lived
Everything we have experienced,
Are experiencing now,
And will experience –
Yet without sin!

Our salvation *and* sanctification
Are both from Him

When the Word speaks to the soul,
There is nothing to contain Him,
Nothing to hinder the gift to the soul

But yet the soul can choose to accept or reject
The greatest Gift of all

Behold, the Word searches for a resting place
Within our souls: will we open the doors
Of our interior lives and let Him enter?

If the doors to our soul
Remain closed, the Lord will never
Leave us, for He has dwelt
Within our souls from the very beginning
Of our existence!

Ah, what happiness immerses the soul
Upon seeing the Word bearing righteousness
From His very heart: the soul desires to accept
This holiness into itself immediately

The Word smiles and gives His heart
To the soul – look, how it bleeds
Mercy and forgiveness!

The Heart of Jesus cleanses all;
Behold, He freely gives Himself
To each one of us

And the soul then speaks
The Word to the Word Himself:
Indeed, the soul proclaims
The most holy name of *Jesus* –
And all things cease, bringing peace
To reign within, by the very power
Of the Word of God!

Wisdom 15

They are better than the objects
They worship

Since You, oh Lord, have made us
Each in Your image and likeness,
Without repeating anyone throughout history,
There is an intrinsic dignity You have bestowed
Upon each of us individually,
And upon humanity collectively as well

For this is a truth, undeniable in nature,
That all men and women are equal to each other
In Your sight, oh God: no one can earn
Your love more than another,
For no one can earn Your love at all

It is Your free gift to us!

Your love is truly unconditional,
Contrasted with our feeble love:
Conditional, fragile,
And at times very selfish

The *gravitas* of our fallen nature
Is felt most profoundly when we love
"Things" above You, oh God,
And take Your love for granted

Oh my Lord and God, the horror
At the mere thought that so many
Believe that they can be defined
By the "things" they have!

Oh my Lord and God, the tragedy
That so many have lived and died
Worshipping "things" instead of You,
Living only for this world
And not for You in the next

The human person cannot be defined
By what things he has,
For these things are temporary, finite –
Even his body will eventually cease,
Decaying after death,
But the immortal soul of man will endure

Turn back to God, and all
Will be satisfied!
Humanity has the capacity
To live for Him, as opposed
To limiting the reception of gifts
To only those which humanity
Can give itself

In the Lord, this blindness
Will be healed – a blindness of heart –
With the Light of Jesus Christ
Shining into our souls

Wisdom 16

To escape from Your hand
Is impossible

Your arms always outstretched,
And Your eyes full of love,
You never leave this position of welcome,
Oh Lord, this invitation to experience
Your love flowing out from Your heart

We may see You there, and walk
The other way – ah, the agony
In their souls unbeknownst to them! –
Will we instead be the Samaritan
To approach You, who are wounded by our sins?

Commit fully to the Lord now,
And experience His hand of mercy
Upon you:
Purification for sanctification

Or if not, what meaning is there to be found?
Experience the Lord's hand of justice
When the tarnished soul *places itself*
Into the fires of hell, while God, in His love,
Puts Himself second
To the soul's disordered priorities:
You love despite the rejection You receive,
Oh Lord

We can either experience the Lord's hand
Here in this life, where the trials of a mortal life
Are as nothing compared with the glory to come,
Or experience the Lord's hand in the next life,
As He shows us the heart we carried
On earth and finds no adherence
To His own

Denying the existence of God
Will not even begin the escape
From Love Himself – to think that a declaration
From humanity could ever change
The nature of God!
How foolish, arrogant,
And dolorous…

But nevertheless there is *always*
Still hope for the reconversion
Of man

Wisdom 17

Wickedness is a cowardly thing

Every choice we make is either
Toward the path of good or evil;
Free will is indeed one of the greatest gifts
The Lord has ever given to us!

A gift indeed, but also
A responsibility

It is difficult to choose the good path many times,
Certainly, but it is not impossible

Fortitude is needed to say no to the ways of the world,
To the ways of sin, and move forward
Towards the Divine,
With Him gently guiding each one of our steps

But wickedness cannot sustain itself,
For it is built upon malice, discouragement,
And ultimately the Devil's evil plans,
Always thwarted by God!

It is cowardice to act wickedly
Because selecting the good path takes courage
And strength from the Lord, and *walking* the good path
Even more perseverance!

By ourselves we can do nothing, and so if we try
To do well by our own efforts we will only succeed
Inasmuch as our human capacity can carry us –
Not very far at all, for charity will gradually
Cease and love be extinguished

But with the power of Jesus Christ, through the working
Of the Holy Spirit, we can approach the Father in humility
As broken sons and daughters needing His love,
And thus He will show us the light
Of the good path without fail,
Without hesitation, without end

Wisdom 18

You called us to Yourself
And glorified us

Behold, humanity together walking
Towards greater things, its members
Individually striving yet somehow one,
With the Lord slowly bringing all
Home to Himself through the gift of death

At that moment of fullness,
Each sees for himself the loving face
Of God, and the judgment each receives
Is both just and merciful – who can stand
Before You, Lord, except that You
Are loving mercy?

The glory of Your likeness You gave to us,
Oh Lord – can such a gift be measured
Or physically perceived? If man is to live at all,
Man must live for You, for by no other way
Can he begin to know himself!

Wisdom 19

So that Your children
Might be kept unharmed

Your embrace, Lord Jesus Christ,
Ignites a fire in our souls – ah, what warmth of life! –
That prepares us, Your children, for Heaven's
magnificence,
If we but accept Your love and live for You…
To You, oh Lord, be glory and praise forever!
Amen! Alleluia!

Part 10

The Heart of Jesus

Fall into the arms of Jesus Christ, the Lord, and let yourself be immersed by His Most Sacred Heart. All of the troubles of your own heart will be assimilated into His Heart, and He will purify the longings of your soul by His gaze of love.

This final poem of the collection *My Soul Longs for You, My God* has a different telos than the rest: while the preceding poems were focused in a certain way on the longings of man as a whole and as individuals, "The Heart of Jesus" is meant only for you, the reader, and for no one else. In other words, the reading of this poem provides the opportunity for the Lord to open your heart and to show you His own.

Therefore, in order to match this poem with its respective introduction, this is an introduction in which the pronoun "you" has been used intentionally. The Lord can speak to you directly, even now, if you but open your heart to Him. God will never force Himself upon you, for He respects your freedom to choose for yourself how to live your life. He can show you over time His plan for you, but you have the capacity to accept or decline this plan. Indeed, how powerful each person is when considered thus, but compared to the omniscient God, how weak and small nevertheless. You are the witness of an incredible paradox:

you are made in the image and likeness of God and thus are His servant, but at the same time have the freedom to act as if you were a king yourself. Embrace the responsibility this entails: live for the Lord, and all of your yearnings will be fulfilled according to His will. This may mean intense sacrifice, even death on the Lord's behalf, but whatever His plan is for you, it is for your greater happiness on the journey to ultimate happiness in heaven with Him.

Behold, the King of the universe approaches you with peace, hope, and love, not violence, despair, and hate. Though the world has given you these horrible things, the Lord will never harm you; the Lord will never abandon you. His heart overflows with love for you, no matter what you have done in your life. It is never too late to return to Him; it is never too late to call Him *Father*, for indeed He is your Father, and He is your God.

God loves you. It is certain that in some way you have heard this statement before. But have you ever paused to ponder its full meaning? The Triune God – Father, Son, and Holy Spirit – has held you in existence your entire life by His love for you. Take a moment to pray about what Jesus is doing for you right now: He is extending to you His Most Sacred Heart, asking you to receive it freely. His heart is for you to keep, for you to treasure always. Will you reciprocate and give Him your heart? The Lord is waiting for you, arms outstretched, with a loving smile. Live for Him the Love He has for you. Go to Him, now and always, with loving joy!

God the Father, embrace us as Your children.
God the Son, have mercy on us, sinners.
God the Holy Spirit, enflame our hearts with Your love.
And Blessed Mother Mary, carry us always to your Son.

Amen.

The Heart of Jesus

Jesus Christ *loves* you

He died for you,
Rose for you,
And perpetually gives you
His own body and blood,
Soul and divinity,
In the Eucharist
For your continued
Sanctification in Him

Enter into the depths of love
Found in the Sacred Heart of Jesus!

Jesus Christ loves *you*

No matter what you have done,
Are doing, or will do in your life,
Either for good or ill,
He will always treasure you
With His entire being,
Keeping you safe from harm
If you allow yourself to be vulnerable
Before Him, like a child

Enter into the depths of love
Found in the Sacred Heart of Jesus!

Jesus Christ loves you!

And you can love Him in return
By giving yourself to Him
With a genuine act of the heart,
Uniting your own with His
Sacred heart for the rest of your life:
To say with millions of souls
Both around the world and in heaven,
"Jesus Christ, I love You!"

Enter into the depths of love
Found in the Sacred Heart of Jesus!

May the Sacred Heart of Jesus
Wash you clean of your sins
By His blood that He shed for you
On the cross

Enter into the depths of love
Found in the Sacred Heart of Jesus!

May the Sacred Heart of Jesus
Bring you closer to the Immaculate Heart
Of Mary, His mother and yours,
And so then she can guide you ever more
To her Son's heart in return:
A mutual love that they hold
For each other,
A love they have for you!

Enter into the depths of love
Found in the Sacred Heart of Jesus!

May the Sacred Heart of Jesus
Increase your charity on earth
To everyone you meet so that
One day you can live with Him
In heaven, continuously
Adoring His Heart pouring forth
Love for you!

Enter into the depths of love
Found in the Sacred Heart of Jesus!

"Jesus, You love me, and I love You!"
This is the exhortation
You are able to give to the entire world –
Truth to be told to every society
To renew every society
In the Truth Himself!

Enter into the depths of love
Found in the Sacred Heart of Jesus!

Jesus Christ loves you *always*!

Enter into the depths of love
Found in the Sacred Heart of Jesus!

Expressions of Gratitude

I would like to thank my parents for their unconditional love, support, and prayers throughout the entire process of prayer, writing, and editing.

I would like to thank the many priests who gave me such spiritual protection and pastoral wisdom through their prayers. I have thanked each one of you personally, but wish to do so again, for without your guidance this project would have been impossible.

I would like to thank all of my spiritual brothers at the seminary who have helped me on this journey. Indeed, all of you have done so with such generous hearts.

I would like to thank all those who, in large and small ways, have carried me to Christ on this journey through prayer and support.

And most of all, it is completely necessary and a joy for me, from the depths of my heart, to thank the Lord for His boundless generosity in choosing me, a sinner, an unworthy servant, to write for Him. Praised be Jesus Christ. Now and forever. Amen.

God the Father, embrace us as Your children.

God the Son, have mercy on us, sinners.

God the Holy Spirit, enflame our hearts with Your love.

And Blessed Mother Mary, carry us always to your Son.

Amen.